IN SEARCH OF MY FATHER

I read with great interest *In Search of My Father,* reliving in many ways some events of my own life. These short stories are more than Clint Toews' boyhood and adult experiences. They are the story of a loving Father constantly looking after us despite our countless adventures away from Him.

As you read this "love story," I hope that the Lord will speak to you as He did to me.

Rev. Bernard Pinet
Provincial Youth Chaplain,
Manitoba, Canada

Clint Toews

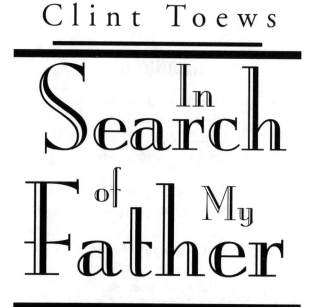

In Search of My Father

The sometimes tender,
sometimes turbulent
chronicles of a young boy's journey.

HORIZON BOOKS

A DIVISION OF CHRISTIAN PUBLICATIONS, INC.
CAMP HILL, PENNSYLVANIA

HORIZON BOOKS

a division of Christian Publications, Inc.
3825 Hartzdale Drive
Camp Hill, PA 17011
www.cpi-horizon.com

In Search of My Father
ISBN: 0-88965-166-3

99 00 01 02 03   5 4 3 2 1

I dedicate this book to the two women without whom
my heart would have remained broken.

My mother,
Peggy,
who nurtured me
with unconditional love and true faith,
and my wife,
Pearl,
my only bride, my confidante,
my dearest friend
and the wind beneath my wings.

Table of Contents

Foreword

To know true sonship is to be known intimately by God the Father. To know the Father-God of the Trinity, one must kneel in humble submission, worship, service and love, with one's whole heart, soul, mind and strength.

Clint has done both—he has knelt before his heavenly Father and he enjoys his sonship.

At the close of the Old Testament, Malachi speaks of turning the hearts of the fathers and their children to each other (Malachi 4:5-6). Later, Luke picks up on this truth when he speaks of John the Baptist having "the spirit and power of Elijah" for turning "the hearts of the fathers to their children" (Luke 1:17).

The spirit and power of Elijah are on this father-writer. Clint has accepted his Father's invitation to enter into His heart as His son. And God has sent the Spirit of His Son into Clint's heart. The result is a turning of Clint not only to his own family, but to other fatherless sons and daughters, helping them discover the Father they never knew.

As you read *In Search of My Father,* you will be invited into the pilgrimage of a son, a man, a father, a grandfather who lost his own dad when he was a young boy. In these pages, you will experience the deep longings of your own soul crying out for your earthly father as you join the author's journey from fatherlessness to being fathered by his eternal God.

Then, as one who has tasted his Father-God's heart, he will let you share in the hope, the forgiveness, the healing and the reconciliation that is all part of God's plan for sons and daughters.

Join Clint in the battle, in his journey of discovery. Catch a glimpse of what it cost him as a son—what it has cost his wife and children—in order to enter into the heart of the Father.

The imprint of God's heart is all over each chapter, each story, each person in this book. As you immerse yourself in these pages, turn toward the Father, that He might imprint you as well. Let His embrace make an eternal mark on your heart, that you in turn may impact still others.

My prayer is that God the Father, "[Who] has made everything beautiful in its time" (Ecclesiastes 3:11), might beautify your heart and life as you read.

A fellow pilgrim and son of the living God,
Steve Masterson, BRE, MA, DD

My Hero
from Afar

In 1981, I wrote a song about my father, Ben P. Toews. The lyrics read:

One day I saw you laughing
The next day you were gone
I tried so hard to kiss you
But it took too long
I tried so hard to follow
the long black car
You were my hero from afar
And you know, you still are.

Chorus
> *You were my hero from afar*
> *You were my hero from afar*
> *You were my bright and shining star*
> *And you know, you know, you still are.*

I'd often lie awake at night
Just to hear the sound
Hoping that your footsteps would come
    around
Waiting for you to hold me
In those strong, strong arms
You were my hero from afar
And you know, you still are.

You are the light of heaven
Upon my aging face
I never met a hero
Who could ever take your place
Your smile tells me a story
Which nothing can erase
You were my hero from afar
And you know, you still are.

1   Father's Son

I coughed once to attract the attention of the plainly dressed receptionist typing medical forms. Her clothes were those of one who does not dress for beauty but rather utility. My mother had said she was an old maid.

I was certain she knew I was there, but she gave no indication of it. Her thin gray hair was pulled back into a roll secured by a large black hairpin. Sitting at her typewriter, straight-backed as she pounded the keys, she was like a concert pianist who never misses a beat, but never bares her soul.

She reminded me a lot of Miss Martha, my teacher. I knew Miss Martha was an old maid because I had asked her. She threatened to give me the strap for being insolent, but instead she made me stay after school to write 100 times, "I will not ask improper questions." When I was done, I still wanted to ask her; I just didn't want to write anymore.

"Why did Miss Martha get mad at me when I asked her if she was an old maid?" I had inquired of my mother.

"Because she once was going to get married, but her husband-to-be changed his mind at the last minute," Mother confided in me. "But don't you say a word about that."

"Why didn't she get another husband?" I pressed on.

"It's not easy when you're heartbroken," was the reply.

My sister Val had told me that "heartbroken" was a thing that ladies got when sad things happened to them. Mostly they cried, but sometimes they got mad. Miss Martha had gotten mad.

The old maid mystery remained as I looked closely at the hospital receptionist. Coming to a typing crescendo with a final thrust of her fingers, she slapped the lever to the left and with one swift motion removed the finished document. Laying it on a pile of other papers nearby, she turned my way, stood and leaned on the counter. Her wire-rimmed glasses framed eyes which scrutinized me as one would survey graffiti on a freshly painted wall.

"Yes?" Half question, half statement, the word directed at me sounded like fingernails on a blackboard.

"I want to see my father," I managed through dry lips, with a higher-than-usual voice.

Without asking who that might be, her answer came at me with the force of a willow switch. "I'm going to call your mother. You are wasting my time. You come here more than the doctors do. Children are not allowed in the hospital," she barked. "You know that, and this is the last time I'll tell you."

Indeed I knew that, but my father-thirst was easily as strong as the vindictive refusal I was encountering. Like a salmon exhausting itself to reach its spawning ground, I plodded up those cold, marble stairs week after week only to be thrown back by the rush and roar of regulation.

Turning away again, I silently and slowly left the place in which my father now lived. A paroxysm of panic clutched at my six-year-old mind. With the powerlessness of a child, I whimpered for God to help me. I was terrified of the growing distance between me and my father. I had been told that God was powerful. I had not seen much evidence of that, but I was also desperate. "Help me see my dad," I murmured under my breath. "I promise not to bug my sisters or steal crab apples or hate Miss Martha." This pretty much covered everything I knew which might be of value to God.

My ears were still stinging with the riot act read to me by the Miss Martha-like woman at the reception desk. I stifled bad thoughts of her and reflected on the incomprehensible system which would keep a son from seeing his father. Rules were nonnegotiable, and a child was usually unheard and underrepresented. Systems were designed for stability, and in the interest of a ripple-free life, humanity was often forgotten. We have come half circle, since we now have humanity without much stability.

My mother had pointed out to me where exactly my father's window was located on the south wall of the Bethesda Hospital in Steinbach. "Go to the tall pine tree on the south side," she had said. "Count up three windows on the southeast corner and two windows on your left. That's your daddy's room."

I ran around the back of the hospital where I could see him if he came to the window. I picked up an acorn and threw it. It bounced off with a ping and fell at my feet. Nervously glancing about lest the hospital handyman see me, I waited for my father to appear. *He must be sleeping,* I guessed. *He'll come tomorrow.*

Reluctantly I crossed the manicured grounds to head home for supper. The October sun was going down early and the shadows were longer these days. I played a solitary game with my shadow. Dodging from side to side, back and forth, I tried to lose it. My teacher had said to me, "You can't have shadows unless you have light." I didn't like shadows—they meant my day was almost over and darkness was coming.

Leaving the hospital grounds, I crossed Hanover Street, kicking a can lying in my path. I walked head down, measuring my progress by the lines in the sidewalk, thinking of the days going by, wondering at the way my life was changing.

Ben had met and married Margaret in the early summer of 1934. Their courtship, by later accounts, was the stuff that stories are made of. He was thirty-five and she was thirty. They were crazy about each other. That was the bottom line.

In those gentler days my father had picked mother up in his Model A Ford as she strolled along a country lane with her sisters. They had literally ridden off together into the sunset. People were grown and prepared for life before they courted in those days and there was little hesitancy for two people in love to embark on life together, and so they did.

Ben was physically powerful, thick-shouldered, blond-haired, blue-eyed, with an easy manner and a musical laugh. He was gentle-natured and kind. Children loved him and approached him when he worked. They seemed to sense instinctively the status he had awarded them and so, when he was unguarded, they often found the throne of his knees.

Margaret adored Ben, who would chase her playfully through the garden, catch her under the apple trees and carry her protesting, but not too vigorously, into the house. She was more self-conscious than he, very pretty, tiny and somewhat anxious. She loved to sing and dance.

Together they built a home and filled it with two daughters and two sons. Ben worked hard loading his 1942 Ford truck with gravel by hand, six loads a day, to re-surface the roads of the municipality. Mother made a home for Ben and the rest of us.

My father, so mother said, was ecstatic when I was born: his first son. I became his shadow, accompanying him on his gravel-hauling trips, playing and watching him while he worked. With great arcing swings of his steel scoop, muscles rippling, sweat pouring, he filled the truck box. He whistled or sang while he worked.

From time to time, my father paused to check up on me. "I want to help you, Daddy," I would say. "I want to shovel too."

"Here you go," he would enthuse, letting me sense my own limitations as he relinquished the great steel shovel to my miniature grasp.

"It's too big, Daddy," and I dropped it.

"So it is," he would say. "We'll get you one your own size."

And one day, stopping at the general store, he accompanied me through the swinging screen door into the dry goods section amid the distinctive smells of tanned leather, salted herring, fresh apples and oiled floors. There I selected a child's shovel to let me become more like him. The image was important; the function was yet to come. His response to my childish desire was essential to my belief that he believed in me.

In the evenings, upon returning home, my mother would rub his feet (a therapy which has eluded the academics), and they would talk about their day. This I watched and learned that touch and talk are important somehow to marriage.

After supper, quite often my father would take his worn baseball mitt and ball in one hand and my hand in the other into the back yard. This was paradise to me. Father's massive, calloused hand would enfold my own as he led me to this school of little information and plenty of relation. "Stand like this," he would say, "rest your bat on your shoulder until you see the ball coming, keep your eye on the ball and then at the right moment, swing." And so my mentoring began and life's mysteries began to unravel under the tutorship of the man I called "Father."

When I hit the ball, Father smiled. Sometimes, only sometimes, he said, "Good for you." He did not badger me with endless explanations nor enthusiasm disproportionate to my accomplishments. He let me savor the moments of my achievement. Life with Ben was as good as it gets.

Slowly things began to change as the summer of 1950 ended. Sometimes my father couldn't go to work. He remained in bed. I would crawl into the truck and shift the gears making engine noises. Then I would return to tell him that I had checked it out and everything was OK for his next trip.

Everything was not OK. Bright's Disease was ravaging my father, and his powerful body was being consumed from within. I was crushed the first time he could not find the strength to play catch. His explanation for me was basic and direct. "Daddy's sick right now, but when I get well, we'll play some more and we'll go to some ball games. Till then, you practice," he said. More wisdom: You do what you can when you can't do what you want to. Others' limitations are not yours, nor the cue for you to stop doing and being your best.

Then one morning Dr. Waters came to examine Father. The doctor looked grim, not his usual friendly self. Soon after, a large car with doors at the back came. They put my dad in a special bed and loaded him into the large car.

"Where are they taking him, Mom?"

"To the hospital." She was crying and could only manage brief explanations.

"When is he coming back?"

"I don't know. Soon, I hope."

"Can I go with him?"

"No. The doctor is going with him."

The car disappeared and I went to sit on his bed. It was still warm.

My foreboding turned into confusion. It covered everything like a pernicious fungus the day they took my father away to become secluded, out of sight and out of reach.

For hours, days and weeks, I practiced bouncing the sponge ball against the cement steps, becoming downright adept at picking up the ricocheting sphere from every angle. I practiced for him. I would show him how I had learned everything he had taught me, show him what I could become. The more I practiced, the sooner he would want to come home. By willing it, it would happen. By doing my best at what I could, I *would* influence his recovery.

Mortality was about to give way to immortality. Understanding neither did not prevent my young heart from the pain of their arrival.

Still heading home from the hospital and in my private thoughts, I was unaware of the presence of my class bully, Branden Sempler, who blocked my path.

"Hey, pip-squeak!" Branden leered at me as bullies do when conditions are just right for domination. A full six inches taller than I was, Branden was obese and unkempt. It was rumored that his father was a heavy drinker and beat him frequently. I lunged to get around him, but his pudgy hands closed on my jacket, ripping it as he flung me to the ground. Sitting on me, he grabbed a handful of mud and dribbled some on my face.

Branden hated me for the usual reasons. I was usually the teacher's pet and excelled at playground games. Girls tried to mother me, and my tendency to compensate for my size with my tongue did not endear me to bullies.

With a mocking laugh Branden pinned me to the ground. His weight drove stones into my back. I was losing my breath.

"You've been to see that stupid, sick father of yours at the hospital again, haven't you?" he sneered. "I hear he's going to die, maybe starve to death. That's what my dad says."

Something synapsed inside me. With the ferocity of a caged beast, I uncoiled like a spring, flinging my tormentor to the side. Volcanic hate spewed out of my soul and I leaped upon him, flailing blindly. Screaming the venom of hell, I assigned to him the curses of the damned, words my father would never have spoken.

I had begun to leave my father before he left me. His wisdom would never hold me to account again.

Leaving the chase, I ran home sobbing. Deep inside me, hope wilted and fear of the future had been distilled into rebellion against anyone who would turn me away, against anyone who would disappoint or reject me, anyone who would try to control me, and against a God who chastises the ones He loves until they know Him too well to leave Him.

The germination of rejection had begun. The combined forces of circumstantial heat, the darkness of confusion and the erosion of trust had split the seed and what was hidden would soon be clearly seen. What a man sows he must reap, but the harvest was many years away.

Mother met me at the door and probed for answers while she held me close. As my grief subsided, I posed my own question to her. "Is Daddy going to die?"

"Oh, I don't think so, my dear."

"Why don't you think so? Branden Sempler says he will."

"Is that what this is all about? Branden doesn't know such things. It was mean of him to say that."

"I hate him."

"You shouldn't hate him. He's a very unhappy boy who has a hard life."

"But his dad isn't sick."

"I know, but his dad doesn't play with him the way yours does."

"You mean the way he *did.*"

She didn't challenge my correction. "Is that why you are so upset? Because of Branden?"

"He hurt me and said my dad would die, but I fought him and he ran."

"Do you think your daddy would want you to fight?"

I was quiet for a moment. "He said that if I couldn't help it, I should fight and not be afraid."

Again she didn't challenge my answer. She rocked me some more, smoothing my hair to the side which boys only allow when they are being rocked by their mothers.

"What if Daddy dies?"

Mother closed her eyes and said nothing as a tear slid down her face.

"Can God make Daddy better?"

She nodded.

"Will He?"

She stared into space and remained silent.

We had both reached the limit of our understanding despite the difference in the years between us. We stood on the level ground of ignorance as the mysteries of God passed before our individual thoughts.

"Come, I'll make you supper." Mothers feed you when they don't have answers for you. It's their way of reassuring those who are left to face their pain. God did it for Elijah. (See 1 Kings 19.) "Eat and sleep," He said as the angel watched over the prophet. "You are too weak for the journey." It's a reflection of God's heart for the confused and overwhelmed.

"Can we have ice cream?" I ventured.

"Ice cream and the chocolate cake I just made," Mother offered.

"I'll save some of mine for Dad," I volunteered.

"It won't keep till he gets home."

I left it anyway.

Winter came early in 1950. The great flood in the spring had consumed the spirit of the people, and summer had passed by almost unnoticed. It was a year of turmoil and catastrophe for the province of Manitoba and for us as a family.

Christmas came. The usual festivities were shrouded in the absence of Father. My teachers, sensing my despondency, tried to brighten the time for me. I was cast in the role of Eleazar, one of the wise men, and got to ride upon one of the larger boys who had been assigned to be my camel. I spent hours making a special Christmas card for my father, depicting him and me on matching camels.

Everything we could spare had been sold to pay for medical bills. The good doctor had decreased his fees, but the cost of Father's prolonged illness finally depleted all we had. I lay for hours under the Christmas tree, looking up at the multicolored lights. There was a lot of room under the tree. Money had become scarce since my father took ill, and Mother was often out waitressing at a local coffee shop or washing office floors to make ends meet.

More relatives came by than usual that Christmas. Often they spoke in muffled tones and often the women cried as they hugged my mother. Uncle Dave, my favorite, came in from Carbelle together with Aunt Agatha.

"Here, kid." He slipped a dollar into my pocket and ruffled my hair. "Don't spend it all in one place." He always said that. But it was one of those things adults say and kids don't understand but they secretly want adults to keep saying. Taking advantage of the presence of the guests, I called out to my mother as I ran out of the door. "I'm going to the store. Be right back!"

Just up the street, the dime store was lit up with colored lights and displays of all sorts. Mr. Kehler, the storekeeper, smiled at me as I entered and said, "Merry Christmas," as he handed me a jawbreaker. Thanking him, I went over to the display of jackknives. Scanning them carefully I focused on one which had an "S" embossed on its green plastic trim. A knife would cheer him up and give him something to do in the hospital. He had carefully shown me how to use a jack-knife on a willow stick. "Always push the blade away from your body," he had instructed. Mr. Kehler came up behind me.

"Is this one made in Germany?" I asked him, pointing to the green-sided knife.

He smiled again, "Why, yes . . . I think it is." Then, "Does your mother know you're buying a knife?"

"Yup," I said, concentrating hard on the knife he was holding.

"Mmmm . . . how much money have you got, young man?" Mr. Kehler often called me that and I liked the way it made me feel. He rested his hand on my shoulder.

"One dollar," I said proudly. Pulling the crumpled bill from my pocket, I showed it to him.

He hesitated, then unlocked the case and carefully withdrew the jackknife. "This one is a Soningen." Mr. Kehler continued, "It's more than a dollar. Is it for you?"

"No, it's for my dad. He's in the hospital, but he needs something to do while he's waiting to get better." Then I took a leap of faith. "He'll pay for the rest when he gets out."

Mr. Kehler's eyes glazed. Finally he said, "Sounds OK to me." He extended his hand and we shook. "It's a deal." He turned away like my mother had when I wanted to save my dessert for father.

Elated at my good fortune, I waited for Mr. Kehler to wrap the knife in tissue and put in into a small green box. Calling out my thanks, I skipped out the door and ran back home. Tucking the knife inside my jacket pocket, I crossed the school yard and turned the corner onto Mill Street. There were several more cars parked on our driveway and in front of the house than when I had left.

An ominous feeling gripped me as I opened the kitchen door. My mother rushed to embrace me. She held me close as if I had been lost. "Your daddy's gone," she whispered and shook with the sadness of one whose grief cannot be contained.

"Daddy's gone?" I repeated.

Pastor Hill placed his hand on my shoulder. His hand was thin and clean, not like my father's. He said, "Your daddy's in heaven. The Lord took him home."

"Home? Which home? Which Lord? What does he mean, Mommy?"

"Daddy's gone to heaven, dear."

I was pinned to the immovable finality of the truth. A rage rose up within me. My soul shook under its strain. "I hate heaven! I hate the Lord! I want my daddy!" Running like an animal before a raging inferno, I fled to my room. Throwing myself on my bed, I cried till my body ached. I lay awake with my clothes on and cried until the sun came up. The frost covered my window, diffusing the morning light. I took out my knife and scratched the words "I love you, Daddy" in the thick frost. It fell cold and wet on my bare feet. The sun shone through the words on my window. By noon the words had disappeared.

Two days later, at 1:30, Pastor Hill pulled onto our yard in his 1950 Dodge. "We're going to the funeral home," my mother announced, picking up my baby brother. "You can come. We're all going together."

"What are we doing there?"

"We're going to see your daddy," she responded dully.

"Why is he there?"

It was too much for her. "Get ready to go. Pastor Hill is waiting."

"You said Daddy went to heaven. Did he come back?"

"Hurry! We'll be late." One of the ironies of being human is hurrying to be a part of something which has no end.

Sitting in the back seat of the car, I listened to the tires splashing through the puddles. We rode in silence except for the sniffing as mother stifled her crying.

Would my father be different? I was afraid to see him dead. Why did people talk quietly when people died? Why did they meet and eat together? Were they afraid too? Was death a way to be together?

The chapel was crowded when we arrived. Some of my uncles stood outside smoking. Uncle Dave ruffled my hair again as I passed him. I checked my pocket for the knife. It was still there.

"I'm going to change your brother. You wait here for me," mother instructed. I looked around me and noticed others were directing furtive glances my way. One lady murmured, "Poor child," as she dabbed her eyes. Why were these people here? Were they my father's friends? There were so many of them.

I had to find my father to see him before he went back to heaven. I walked to the front of the chapel and pushed aside a heavy velvet curtain. Before me was a door marked "antechamber." Having been taught by my sisters to read by the age of five, I was able to sound out the words, although I could not understand their meaning.

Pushing open the door, I saw in the soft light a coffin on a trolley. A spray of daffodils lay at the foot. As my eyes grew accustomed to the dim light, I discerned the profile of a man's face. "Daddy," I whispered, "I came to see you." The man in the casket did not resemble my father, but I knew it was him. There are things which cannot be taught and some which cannot be unlearned.

Using a stool nearby, I stepped up to look into the face of my father. They had taken away his leather airman's jacket. It used to pillow my head as I would fall asleep on late trips home from the gravel pit. He would spread the jacket out for me on the truck seat and, with his one hand on me, sing until I drifted off.

Now he was dressed in a pin-striped suit of itchy cloth which smelled like soap. Still, I put my head down on him. His massive chest was gone. His eyes were closed, his hands were thin and white like Pastor Hill's. Did death change people into strangers? I wept in broken confusion. "Good-bye, Daddy. You'll always be my daddy." My tears cut rivulets through the undertaker's chalk as I kissed him. "What will I do without you?" I lamented. "What will I do tomorrow?" I lay on his unmoving body until the door opened.

"I've been looking all over for you." Mother's voice shook with emotion as she added, "Say good-bye to Daddy. We have to go now."

I slid to the floor and my hand closed over the knife again. "I bought this for you," I said quietly as I slipped the Soningen into his pocket. "It's made in Germany."

A dull ache throbbed in my chest as I closed the antechamber door behind me. The last few grains of sand passed through the hour glass. Tomorrow we would turn it over. Life without Ben had begun.

For weeks I said little. What's to say when someone takes your life away? That would change in time, but in the antechamber of my heart, my father would lie in state for years to come. And for all those years I did not bury him.

2 When the Winds
of Heaven Blow

I watched the huge, diesel moving truck inch its way along our gravel drive, pulling two huge beams upon which sat our garage.

One by one we had sold our assets to pay medical bills during my father's illness, and the garage was the last to go. First the trucks, then the tools, and on this unspeakable afternoon a mover had come to haul our double garage away.

It had been my cathedral in which I worshiped my father. I spent hours just listening and watching him work on his trucks or tinker with this or that or talk with his friends. His belly laughs echoed off the shiplap walls while

19

he spun yarns of his dealings with Winnipeg's scrap merchants. When he wasn't hauling gravel, he was hauling scrap iron. Now a stranger was hauling away what remained of my life with him, the scraps of our few years together.

I watched the truck and garage disappear up Mill Street. When they were gone I returned to the empty square of oil-stained gravel where my dad's truck had parked. The oil seemed like a bloodstain on the ground. For weeks I took a detour to school in order to pass the house where our garage now stood. I even went inside once, but no trace of my father remained. It was my last effort to keep with me what had been his.

My mother was a lover of creativity. It showed in the way she dressed her children. Soon after dad's death, however, clothes were made, not bought, or inherited from others, not ordered from the catalog.

One day news came that my friend Claude, who had been sick all winter, had died. Mixed in with my sadness at losing him was an envy that Claude would see my father before I would. Then it was revealed that the box my mother brought home from her visit to Claude's mom contained my dead friend's clothes, including his long underwear, now to become mine.

A mixture of grief and embarrassment coursed through me as I sat on the edge of my bed, not daring to look into the mirror. Already I despised myself for being poor. I wanted to be someone else at that moment. An eerie sense of being somehow clothed for death pervaded my thoughts. I remained motionless there in my room, as a rabbit crouches trembling in an open field, hoping his enemies will not see him. Then mother called from the hallway, "We're leaving for church now."

Each week I dreaded that announcement. The mile walk, with a stiff white shirt collar chafing my neck, was a marathon of misery, especially in winter. Then we sat immobilized on hard benches while old men spoke in melancholy tones in a language I did not understand. Once during each meeting ushers handed around the collection bag for money offerings. My friend Andy put tape on his fingers one Sunday and got out more coins than he put in. Later he told me his father had cried as he whipped him for stealing God's money.

It seemed to me that if we put money into God's bag, He should share it with us quite willingly since He owned everything. Mom said all we had came from God, even Claude's clothes, and that I should be thankful for them. All I was sure of was that if I had been God, I would have given me a new wardrobe and a new Chicago Black Hawks hockey uniform. With new Johnny Bauer skates and stick just to be generous.

When they dismissed the children to attend Sunday school class, I kept my coat on over Claude's clothes and sat as far away as I could from the heat register. Mr. Felcher, our teacher, stood ramrod straight before us, calling for order. With a voice rarely used in his solitary work as a librarian, he was unsuited for his role as our teacher. We sensed his timidity and tested his tolerance.

There had been a question percolating in my mind in my current obsession with death. Now I asked it without hesitation. "Why did Jesus raise people from the dead if they had to die again anyway?"

Mr. Felcher fidgeted, looking nervously up from his lesson book. "I don't know, Clint. We're not talking about that right now. This lesson is about Paul's missionary journey to Ephesus and other cities in Asia Minor."

Undeterred by his correction, I persisted. "Is that why Jesus cried before He raised Lazarus up from the grave, because He knew he'd have to die again?"

"If you don't stop interrupting the lesson you'll have to stand outside the door."

Momentarily silenced, I contented myself with filling in all the O's in my work manual, drawing skates instead of sandals on a picture of the Apostle Paul, adding a hockey stick in his hand.

Teachers everywhere had begun to dread my presence in their classes—as well as my insatiable curiosity, to say nothing of the mischief I brought with me.

Glancing up from my doodling, I noticed Mr. Felcher glaring at me. "Are you listening to me? This is today's memory verse. 'My God shall supply all your need according to his riches in glory by Christ Jesus.' Philippians 4:19. Repeat it after me."

And we did. "My God shall supply all your need according to his riches in glory by Christ Jesus. Philippians 4:19," we chorused.

Just words strung together in an obligatory chant. The reality of their truth was to become mine not many hours later, God's personal words to a searching soul.

Since I was a child I have had the urge to impact the people I am with. A prophetic character, however immature, must make itself heard. So I circled back to the lesson at hand and spoke out of turn again.

"Mr. Felcher."

"Yes." He did not look up this time.

"I heard that Paul the Apostle was an American."

Mr. Felcher glared at me through glasses which made him look beady-eyed, giving him, with his long neck, the appearance of a turtle. When frustration rose within him, a large vein stood out on his forehead and he developed a tick which caused his Adam's apple to move up and down his neck. All three signs were present as he now spoke.

"The Apostle Paul was not an American, not even an American Jew. He was a Jerusalem Jew, and now you'll have to stand in the hallway."

"If I can prove it," was my quick response, "can I stay?"

He hesitated suspiciously. "All right, go ahead."

I continued, "He said he had learned, in whatever state he was, to be content." Loud guffaws filled the room.

"That's enough. Out to the hall. I'll be speaking to your mother."

My foot landed on my friend Barry's toe as I left, causing him to yelp in pain. My teacher reached for me but I eluded him, turning sideways as I slid out of the door.

Energetic and overly restricted by a cautious mother, I constantly tested boundaries. More than this, if the truth be known, I found religious exercises of any stripe to be unimaginative, boring and somehow irrelevant to the real world.

Listening at the Sunday school class doorway, I heard Mr. Felcher begin chorus time. It was the only part of Sunday I loved.

My buddy, Les Hamm, asked to sing "Rudolph the Red-Nosed Reindeer." As I peered in the window I saw Rudolph Ginter, sitting beside him, punch him hard. Les had no dad either.

"OK, we'll sing 'Climb, Climb Up Sunshine Mountain,' " intoned Mr. Felcher.

They began,

> Climb, climb up sunshine mountain,
> Heavenly breezes blow.
> Climb, climb up sunshine mountain,
> Faces all aglow.
> Turn, turn from sin and doubting
> Looking to the sky.
> Climb, climb up sunshine mountain,
> You and I.

They finished, and I made a mental note to ask Mr. Felcher what heavenly breezes were next Sunday. The bell sounded, signaling the end of classes. Leaving quickly, I found mother settling down for the service in the main sanctuary.

"How was Sunday school?" She knew me well, and she watched my eyes closely for signs of deception. Mother had told me the eyes were windows of the soul and revealed hidden secrets. That was why I usually looked elsewhere while answering her questions.

"Sunday school was OK," I mumbled.

Mother was not satisfied. "What was the lesson about?"

I groped for snippets of stories I had garnered from previous lessons, stringing them together. "Well," I began, "God threw Paul off his horse so after that he had to walk all over as a missionary to Asian miners. When he got tired of walking he took a ship which was wrecked by a hurricane to the Ephesians. But he rescued everyone with the help of an angel and lived on an island of rattlesnakes where the Romans put him in jail and chopped off his head."

My mother turned her face to hide a smile brought on by my enthusiastic but incoherent rendition of early church history.

"That must have been a very exciting lesson indeed. I think I'll ask Mr. Felcher whether he and I are reading the same Bible."

I sensed trouble. "Want to hear my Bible verse?"

Mother had a grade five education but handed out verses for us to memorize every morning at breakfast at home. Knowing my verses was at least equal to getting an A in her books.

"My God shall supply all your need according to his riches in glory by Christ Jesus. Philippians 4:19," I declared.

"Very good. Do you know what it means?"

"It means when we run out of money God finds a way to share His with us."

It was truth born in the imagination of a child and anointed by the Spirit of truth. It was good enough for mother, and that pleased me.

"Mom?"

"Uh-huh?"

"What are heavenly breezes?"

"I don't know. Where did you hear about them?"

"We sing about them in Sunday school."

"Well, I think they are winds from heaven God sends to earth to help people, maybe sailors who can't get home."

"Was the wind that wrecked Paul's ship a wind from heaven?"

"Maybe you could ask Mr. Felcher."

I had already decided to do that. So I went on to my more immediate concerns.

"Are you going to give away our money to the church today?"

"Yes I am. There's a special offering for the lepers today. Mr. Tanner is showing pictures of his work among them in Africa."

My face fell. I knew Mr. Tanner and others like him only as those who depleted my mother's meager resources. Every time a missionary visited our church we ate macaroni for a week.

"Don't give any money tonight, Mom."

"I have to, Clint."

"Why? God doesn't need our money. He can give them some of His."

"Listen to me. The Bible says God is no man's debtor. He makes sure He gives you more than you give Him, but His gifts are not always money."

I couldn't think of one that wasn't. I also knew that most times when I asked for something I was told there was no money for it. I was more than certain that if mother gave the $5 she had crumpled in her hand, the hockey stick I wanted for Christmas would end up in Mr. Tanner's pocket.

"What's a leper, Mom?"

We watched as Mr. Tanner ascended the stairs to the pulpit. The large pockets on his black suit must be where he kept the money from his meetings.

"Is a leper like a leprechaun?"

"No, of course not. It's a person with a very serious disease that makes his fingers and toes fall off."

"Is Mr. Reamer a leper?"

"No, he's a carpenter who sawed off his fingers by accident. Now be quiet."

The meeting finished and mother gave her last $5 to Mr. Tanner. In my mind God took more than He gave. I was sure of that.

The Widow's Allowance check was our main source of income. This governmental mercy came to us once a month; we all knew the exact day it would arrive and all purchases were gauged by that day.

At supper my mother took me aside and sat me down. It was like an audience with the queen; she only took one of us aside on very special occasions. "Your brother is sick," she began. "You'll have to pick up the check at the post office. Be extra, extra careful. It's all we have for Christmas."

My mouth went dry as my mission became apparent to me. I was a spy. I had to go behind enemy lines and make it safely home again. There was no room for error. No second chance. Christmas and all it would or wouldn't be came to rest on my eight-year-old shoulders. I felt adventurous and scared at once.

"Can't you ask Uncle Roy to go?" I asked.

"No, he's got the flu," Mom replied.

Slowly I dressed, then, bundled and bent, I trudged, head down, into the darkness and the driving snow. It felt eerie. The snarling wind seemed to become angrier at my appearance. No shortcuts tonight. I was staying under the streetlights.

Fifteen minutes later I entered the warmth of the village post office. Brushing crusted snow from my face and tongue, I looked through the tiny window in box 244. There it was, brown and official, stamped "Government of Canada." A feeling of power and privilege came over me as I slid it underneath my jacket. I was in charge of our money. My mother needed me and I would not disappoint her. Pressing my right hand against my jacket, I felt the check over my heart.

I murmured a mantra of concentration as I hurried homeward. "Christmas money, keep it safe, Christmas money, keep it safe, Christmas money . . ." and soon my overshoes kept rhythm and my buckles sounded like jingle bells.

I turned up our driveway, calling out as I mounted the snow-covered steps, "I got it, Mom, I got . . ."

My voice trailed off, then rose like the wail of a banshee at what happened next. As I moved my right hand to open the door handle, the precious envelope fell, but did not make it to the ground before it was wind whipped into the night.

Mother came running and knew the truth as she saw the abject horror on my tortured face. Bending she took my shoulders, looking down into my face. "Listen to me."

Her words became the gift which money could not buy and remain cast in my memory today.

"You go look for the check, and I'll pray."

True words of faith are hard to come by. They are easily spoken outside of testing trials. Those which cross the lips of trusting saints at those times are pure gold. They are as rare as finding a needle in a haystack—or an envelope on which your life depends in a howling prairie storm.

The door closed behind me, and I turned to face the cold night wind by faith—Mother's faith. My footsteps dragged me into the place where only God could help me or Mother.

She had laid down the terms of this venture. *You look; I'll pray.* "Seek and ye shall find."

So I walked. "Climb, climb up sunshine mountain, heavenly breezes blow. Turn, turn from sin and doubting, looking through the snow . . ."

At the head of our driveway I leaned fatigued and faithless against a wooden utility pole. Sinking to the ground, I heard the sound of paper bending. Straining in the darkness, my eyes saw, stuck in a crack of the pole, my mother's precious check. I seized it with the hunger of a starving child. Heavenly breezes were a mystery no more. The certainty of God's provision was indisputable to me. An angel with cold hands smiled at a little boy who ran home shouting, "I got it! I got it! Mother, I got it!"

The angel turned to look at the Father, "He believes, doesn't he?"

"Oh yes! He believes," came the reply. "It often happens when the winds of heaven blow."

3   The Father-
Heart Fraternity

There is found throughout societies everywhere a fraternity of men with father-hearts who shine with welcoming light to guide those who wander in the darkness of fatherlessness. The love they give goes beyond the borders of their own family or social standing. When God said that He sets the lonely in families (Psalm 68:6), I believe He also had these kind of men in mind.

Among their number were several who fathered me between the ages of nine and sixteen. All of them are now old or gone. They have heard my gratitude for doing for me things my father could not. Some gave callouses to my hands to elevate me to endurance; others spoke words of consolation in times of grief or gave wisdom for direction. Still others held me to account for deeds unbecoming integrity.

Why did they do it? I have asked the question of each one. Most didn't know—maybe it was an instinct similar to nurture. One said he didn't think he had a choice; he would have wanted someone to do it if his own son were fatherless. Whatever their reasons, these men were like lighthouses unmoving, shining in the storm. They marked the rugged shoreline of my life, and they were my fraternity of fathers.

Mr. Penfold was one of these. Program director at a summer camp I attended, he noticed I was not appearing for my daily ration of oranges at the camp store. Without a dollar of my own, I busied myself with other things as the rest of the children lined up to purchase their fruit. However, Mr. Penfold accurately read my disappointment. Calling me to the privacy of his office, he invited me to pick up my oranges each day at the director's cabin, free of charge. Showing me this favor removed the stigma of poverty and gave me instead the status of privilege. It confirmed the value I deeply desired in the eyes of a fatherly man.

The prophet Isaiah describes the father-heart this way: "Come, buy wine and milk without money and without cost" (Isaiah 55:1). I got oranges. Milk, wine and oranges are all perishables; a father's generosity is not. Mr. Penfold is a theologian, preacher and author. With all due respect to him, I cannot remember much of what he wrote, taught or preached. But I remember his kindness, and I was changed by it. His simple act of kindness at a strategic moment anchored my belief in love, his love and the love of the God he believed in. He was a member of the Father's Fraternity.

Fathering cannot be done selfishly. Its effect is filtered by its motivation. If I spend "quality" time with my child and my busy mind is elsewhere when I do, I have spent no time with him at all. If I do so simply because I want him to turn out OK or not give the family trouble, his spirit will pick it up like radar. To take its fatherly effect, "love must be sincere" (Romans 12:9). The timbre of the father's heart is unconditional love. Only Father God can offer that. Only we can receive it.

At the corner of Mill Street and Friesen Avenue, one block from my childhood home, stood a large house with a spacious yard bordered by gnarled maple trees. Mother allowed me to walk the block to this place each Saturday to watch some of the older neighborhood boys play rugby—a game she prayed I would never play. Pick-up games were organized by choosing sides. Teams were formed by selecting the best players first. The least athletic were left to be chosen last. I was too young to be picked at all, but I lived each throw, catch, kick and run. To say I was obsessed by sport would be to understate the truth.

Then one day I worked up the courage to ask the most athletic player who owned the football and lived in the big house whether I could play. A chorus of "no way" rose up from all who had gathered to play—except from the one to

whom I had appealed. I stood before him as one would before a judge. The skinny kid looking up at him offered him
nothing. In fact I represented a liability to his team. There
was silence as I and everyone else waited for my idol's answer. The muscular one put his arm around my shoulders
and drew me into the circle of his team. "Of course you can
play," he said. That was the papal decree, and I played that
wonderful day.

He did more than gather me in. He taught me the
game, applauding my progress. Thereafter he made it
known to all the boys that I would have access to his football, stored in the porch of his house, any time I wanted it.
That first summer I almost wore out his football and over
the years I became an accomplished player. I owe a debt of
gratitude to a young man in the prime of youth who was
not too self-absorbed to allow and encourage a skinny kid
to catch up to him, who gave to his own disadvantage and
inspired an awkward child to seek the excellence of his
dreams.

Lorne's instruction and inclusion of me was the Father-
Heart Fraternity at work. He was captain of my Team of
Fraternal Fathers.

I had three uncles who taught me the fulfillment of
work. There are those who still believe that the curse pronounced on mankind in the Garden of Eden was the curse
of work. In fact, it was not work but the nature of that
work. Faced with an uncooperative environment, man
would have to struggle to perform the redemptive task of
working. My three uncles demonstrated the value of wis-

dom, tolerance, excellence and persistence in work. They expected me to make mistakes and learn from them.

In the Psalms, King David prays to God, "Establish thou the work of our hands" (90:17, KJV). He does not explain how he believes God will do this. In my life I think God used two of my uncles in particular to do it. In the wisdom of their collective years it strikes me that without exception they must have recognized my fatherless ineptitudes.

In the days of which I speak, boys of nine, ten and occasionally younger drove farm tractors. Almost all boys by the age of twelve had a basic knowledge of mechanical or carpentry tools and the skills to go with them. They also knew why things did or didn't work. They knew how and why things were built, bought or bartered. By the time they married, they were prepared to maintain, develop or renovate their homes. These axioms of skillful confidence had been imparted to them by their fathers.

A father taught his son how to work, and that work defined not him but his contribution to a safe, solid and successful society. Those with father-hearts did not stop at the function of work. They clothed all function with a relationship of moral character. The heart and mind were taught to sing the song of manhood and fatherhood in harmony.

Uncle John took unusual risks when he installed me, an untutored fourteen-year-old town boy, on his WD 45 Allis Chalmers tractor and turned me loose to plow his field. I sat enthroned high above the ground, feeling for all the world like Lawrence of Arabia on his sleek steed, ready to charge across the desert. Alas, a saddle doth not a rider make. Twenty minutes after my coronation I had buried my trusting uncle's plow hitch deep in prairie gumbo.

He came to extricate me and had me continue. Things improved. Then in the glow of setting sun I returned like a conquering general from the battlefield. Dusty but delighted, I wheeled through the gate and across the yard where Uncle John and Aunt Elizabeth stood, milk pails in hand, awaiting my arrival.

Flushed with success, I waved at them as a dignitary might greet the crowds who had come to view his procession. My total preoccupation with the glories of farming was interrupted by the looks of consternation crossing the faces of my audience. A split moment later the tractor undercut the gasoline storage tank with a splintering crash, catapulting me skyward and then, in thudding disgrace, onto the ground. The WD 45 continued on broadside into the garage beyond me. Then all was still except for my moaning of pain and shame at the foot of my grand disaster.

Suddenly an uproariously throaty laugh filled the barnyard, drowning out my own cries as my uncle, tears of mirth flowing down his face, came to pick me up. My aunt screamed her dismay and frustration, but my uncle John and I worked till dark to repair all things broken. The next day he sent me out again, a loser in the battle but a winner in the war. Uncle John was a general and father of the Fraternity.

The Irish had nothing on my uncle Ernie. His eyes hardly ever stopped smiling. They teased me but their clear message to me was "You're all right, young man." I liked working for him. Quite simply, it seemed that he expected me to succeed at whatever he gave me to do in his construction business. When I didn't, he always had a positive way to correct matters. I recall burying his gravel truck up to its axles in a swamp we were attempting to fill.

He said little when I phoned for help but came quickly to my rescue. A farmer nearby came to lend a hand with his enormous tractor. Uncle Ernie focused on the amazing towing power of the massive machine. He turned my embarrassment into excitement. He could have ranted and raved at the cost and inconvenience my carelessness had caused, but he let me learn in dignity from my mistakes. It is highly doubtful that my uncle needed an inexperienced Elvis Presley look-alike whose mind was on girls most of the time. Still, he gave me a job whenever he could. He was my father's youngest brother and the older brother of my Father Fraternity.

It was hard to be indifferent about Uncle Ben, even for a ten-year-old boy. He just wasn't like most old people I knew who kind of drifted through my life, talking about politics and money, going to weddings or funerals and looking serious most of the time.

Uncle Ben was a character who overshadowed his age classification. He knew my real name wasn't "Cliff." My name was not all that common, and most people, especially some of the older ones, didn't get it right. I even had to explain several times at high volume to one old fellow that my name wasn't "Click."

Uncle Ben called me Clint. Sometimes with a mischievous twinkle in his eye he would call me Fritz Franz Noodle Soup! If I dropped in at his creamery after school, which was every other day in summer, he usually came up with a fudgesicle.

When I was just a kid, he let me steer his 1952 DeSoto during Sunday rides in the countryside. My mother vigorously protested from the back seat, but she was overruled by Uncle Ben's matter- of-fact explanation, "Well, Peggy, he's just a boy and boys need to know about cars." Who could argue with logic of that caliber?

Life has its ironies. One irony is that when you are young with plenty of time to spend, you have little money and when you are old and have the money, you are running out of time. I was not poverty-stricken in the strict sense of the word, but most of my clothes were hand-me-downs. (That can be embarrassing when your oldest siblings are sisters!) To buy the absolute necessities of life like marbles, firecrackers and bubble gum cards, I collected bottles. Saturday mornings were spent combing the ditches along Highway 12 just outside of Steinbach, my hometown, looking for Friday night's throwaways. Winters were tough and my bottle harvest was meager—until I hit the mother lode of the bottle refund industry.

Coming home from Elmsdale School one afternoon, I took a shortcut behind Mr. Barkman's dry goods store and came upon a treasure trove of bottles stacked high in wooden crates. It was like winning a bottle lottery or, in my case, a lot of bottlery.

Surveying the mass of bottles, I mentally converted it into the world's largest bubble gum card collection, bar none. I had become the Nelson Rockefeller of the bottle return industry. With my heart pounding, I imagined the instant popularity which would surely be mine upon coming to school with not one Rocket Richard card but a handful of the rare ones. I would be king of the pack. What a winter this would be!

The next day I began to cash in my bottles. As fast as Mr. Barkman carried them out the back door, I hauled them in the front. This was Steinbach's first recycling project. My bubble gum trading stock rose to incredible heights overnight. At one point I owned four Harry Lumleys, five Rocket Richards and six Terry Sawchuks.

In addition to my material wealth, great relational favor became mine and I began to receive many side benefits. I had access to all Larry Bowers' comic books, the use of a hockey suit for Saturday afternoon road hockey and considerable freedom from homework.

Then as quickly as it had come, it left me. I know what the miners in California felt like when the gold rush was over. Mr. Barkman had done his research and found a leak in the system. He stopped it by hiring me one afternoon to stack all those bottle cartons in his storage room!

Bent but not broken, I returned to my Saturday morning salvage operation. The stock market had crashed and my winter wonderland became no-man's-land once again.

Spring came and with it the inevitable talk of summer camp. I wanted to go badly. Even talk of Matilda, a large girl in my class who had a crush on me and was going to camp, couldn't diminish my desire. Matilda felt motherly toward me inasmuch as I was a very small boy for my age. When they took choir pictures at school, I was always the one at the end of the front row. There *were* some advantages to being small, like riding the "camel" in the Christmas play.

But one of the disadvantages of being small was being unable to reach the water fountain. Matilda once held me up while I drank, but she lifted me too high and I got water on my trousers. One of the hardest things I've done is trying to dry my pants on a wall dryer while wearing them.

As school days slipped by, I became increasingly focused on camp. I would do anything to go. Secretly, I told my closest friends that I would kiss Matilda on the mouth in public if it would bring me my camp money. The collection of money to sponsor this spectacle began with vigor but I recanted before recess as I could not bear the thought of such humiliation. So another scheme came into being.

My friend, big Adolf Gunter, had an idea. "We will give you five bucks if you sing completely off-key at the music festival," he said, "and another two bucks if you change the words of your song to say, 'Early one morning just as the sun was rising I heard Mr. Friesen burping in the valley below.'"

Adolf really had some dumb ideas, and anticipating corporal punishment drove me to refusal. Summer was coming closer, and the thought of profound boredom while my friends sat around campfires by night and chased screaming girls with leeches by day was becoming increasingly unacceptable to me.

I tried the Bible memorization program. Searching diligently for verses under five words produced a mere twenty or so. Why were the prophets so long-winded, anyway? Why could I memorize the complete rosters of six NHL clubs but reach mental paralysis after twenty Bible verses? I reflected on this fact and decided to make a vow: "Oh Lord, I'll never flick paper spitballs off the church balcony at Mr. Packer's bald head ever again."

But then it occurred to me that God probably wanted me to go to camp anyway to become a better behaved Christian, so He would help me with memorization even if I didn't keep my vow.

The next morning I found, to my mixed delight and sadness, that my favorite girlfriend was going to camp. That settled it. If there was any hope of showing her how I could hit a baseball into the blueberry patch behind left field at the camp ball diamond, it was time here and now to get financially serious.

It is at this point that Uncle Ben reenters my story. Uncle Ben smiled his usual mischievous smile when he opened the screen door for me. "Who have we here?" he asked. "Have you come to eat some fresh buns?"

Heaven knows fresh buns were definitely one of my priorities, but my courage in coming was fueled by other issues. Uncle Ben had very little education but a whole lot of wisdom. When he said, "Who have we here?" he was able to communicate welcome, delight and personal value all in one four-word phrase.

"Have you got a job for me?" I blurted out. I thought about running before he said no.

"I think I can manage that," he said, reading my expression.

My heart beat faster. "You can?"

His next comment drove home the reality of my immediate future employment. "You can weed the garden."

That was right up there with, "Come in and do your homework!" I had thought that he might want a chauffeur to steer his '52 DeSoto to the creamery where I would spend the rest of the afternoon sorting fudgesicles. Anything. But not weeding.

But, alas, Uncle Ben led me through the garage and into the backyard. Confronting me was a sight that would "de-fudgesicle" the mind of any ten-year-old fortune hunter. A sea of Canadian Thistle, Burning Pigweed, Creeping Charlie, Shepherd's Purse and a variety of other joyless plants lay before me. "Clean it and you've got ten bucks," offered Uncle Ben.

It was a fortune by any standard, but only visions of me with a Louisville Slugger in my hands and a ball landing smack in the middle of the blueberry patch drew me into the jungle. I stepped forward and a convention of mosquitoes circled my head. I killed two and fourteen came to the funeral. Why hadn't Noah killed the two he had on the ark?

Pulling plants with a vengeance, I moved like Popeye through the garden. Nettles stuck in my hands, sweat mixed with dust and muddied my face. My throat was parched dry. By 5 o'clock I was done. The garden was bare. Every weed—and vegetable—lay on a limp pile in one corner. I had done exactly what Uncle Ben had asked me to do. I had cleaned his garden out completely!

I walked up the back steps and knocked on the screen door to call Uncle Ben for the inspection. He surveyed the empty patch for a long time, his kind eyes taking in the devastation before him. Poking his teeth with a piece of milkweed, he gave no visible signs of a man who had just been sentenced to a winter of canned, store-bought vegetables. Then he spoke. "My dear boy, you have worked very hard!"

A beaming smile of pride covered my face. I had secured the admiration of a man I greatly wanted to please. He said nothing of my misplaced zeal. Quite apart from the fact that he sacrificed his irritation and loss that day to protect my self-respect and will to work, Uncle Ben paid me twice as much as he had promised.

That summer I went to camp. I heard about mercy, grace and loving-kindness, and I thought about the weed garden more than once. When I was thirty-five, Uncle Ben told me the truth about the weed garden. Those weeds grew back quickly, but my respect for Uncle Ben grew more quickly. I don't recall a single sermon from my uncle, but he taught me about God's mercy, goodness and grace in a way I can never forget.

I'd like to pay Uncle Ben back, although he's gone now. I think I will, in the same way he paid me. He was the president of my Father Fraternity.

4   Grandpa's Hands

Grandfather lived in the corner of a parking lot. At night the large lampposts shone over his fence, making it seem as if the moon were in his backyard. We kids loved it. He had refused to sell his 2,000-square-foot property to the car dealership bordering his homestead. So the lot was built around him and at a level which caused flooding in Grandpa's yard each spring. He said nothing but built wooden sidewalks to use till the water went down. He would say that all that muddy water left good soil behind for his garden, which occupied most of his front yard. "Why waste the space on a crop you can't eat? A lawn is all work and no food."

Behind his miniature brick-siding house was Grandpa's workshop, a place of wonderment to me. I watched him work for hours after school and on Saturdays. Grandpa was no talker but he was a real thinker. Talking is easier but the results are quite different.

He was an inventor too. On his kitchen counter sat a machine he invented for shaping metal, a lathe of sorts. When Grandma died, his kitchen became an extension of his workshop. Like most kids, my interrogation of him was of the endless variety, comprised of one basic question followed by a whole series of "whys" to his responses.

"Grandpa, why can I go faster on my bike when my legs don't even move as fast as when I'm running?"

"Because of your bicycle gears, son."

"Why?" and so on and so on.

Grandpa Sawatsky's ancestors had joined an army in Eastern Poland, generations ago, to fight against the invasion of Genghis Khan. Led by certain nobles, they repelled the attack at a river crossing. Thereafter, they had been called Sawadskys, "sawada" for river and "sky" for an inherited noble designation. The symbol of the clan was a dagger. Somewhere along their historical journey they joined the Mennonite stream and the dagger was suppressed as too violent an instrument to represent them.

Grandpa was an enigma to many in the highly structured religious and social setting in which he lived. Inventive and independent, he cut his own course in life, refusing to join causes, churches or cooperatives. He did attend church without joining it for some years. When my mother was a child she had become quite ill with influenza one Christmas. One of fifteen children, she was unable to get the medicine she needed. Grandpa approached an elder of his church who owned a grocery store for a dozen oranges on credit. His request denied, Grandpa never darkened the door of a church until his funeral. He simply would not accept the leadership or ministry of those who betrayed their own values. He also abhorred senseless legalisms.

A group of Mennonites had decided to flee governmental school control by emigrating to Mexico in the early 1900s. Grandpa saw an opportunity to establish his family on cheap land in Mexico. His brothers-in-law also worked on persuading him to go.

The day of departure came. Families gathered at the train station. Pulling up in a wagon loaded with baggage and kids, Grandpa was told, "You can come to Mexico with your family but your mustache stays behind!"

Apparently great handlebar mustaches were not considered to be self-effacing enough and might jeopardize Grandpa's humility. His reaction was typical: "If my mustache is that important, I'm heading in the wrong direction," he said, whereupon he turned the horses around and headed for home.

There were other times when the message was clearly given to me by him: Property versus people is no contest. You are not your brother's keeper, but you are his brother.

On Sundays he would sit outside his house on a stylish wooden bench he had made. Excellence was his code. Dressed in his pinstriped wool suit, summer or winter, he quietly sat observing, listening. I would sometimes sit beside him. One day I asked him, "Grandpa, what are you doing here?"

"I'm praying," he answered.

Prayer in a garden. A freeing thought to be sure.

With no father and no workshop of my own, I went to Grandpa's place to watch what a man did with his hands. An accomplished carpenter, mason, inventor, gunsmith, artist, tinsmith, tailor and mechanic, Grandpa was an astounding jack-of-all-trades and master of several. Watching him, one could quite easily come to believe that anything is possible for those who believe it is.

To every man who has found himself short of words in this world, let it be said that your hands can achieve what no words could hope to. There are essential words—simple words of love, encouragement and instruction—which cannot be replaced. But as one who has spoken far too many words, I believe men who lead with their hands are rare and precious indeed. Your example and your attitude, overall, will tell your dear ones who they are to you and who you are to them.

How very fortunate the child or wife is who watches a man faithfully build a balanced and stable home, confirming by words born out of silence, the loving work of his hands. Not exclusionary silence: careful silence, the creative place for well-timed words of wisdom and love like apples of gold.

Words are overrated. I believe this, even as a writer. We live under a waterfall of words. Media has become the mecca to which society pilgrimages. We run the gauntlet of advertising signs to and from work. Our athletes are billboards in motion. We have built a tower of "babble," and our society is not the better for it.

My grandpa's conversations were thoughtfully measured. Mother said in her lifetime she had not heard him deprecate anyone with his words. He shot only with his guns. So to every man who shelters his family with the affirmation of his hands, I say bless your skills, bless your inventions, bless your strength and bless the sweat of your brow.

Today children long to be taught by a father who will patiently share the practical things of his life, who will wade through the ineptitudes of his children, welcoming them to share his skill and knowledge. You, sir, whoever you are, believe this. You have what it takes, you have what kids want, no matter what it looks like. If your attitude is love, you are a pied piper in the making. It will happen sooner or later if you don't quit.

Sadly, Grandpa let me watch and learn but he never let me try. If he had, it would have changed my life in many ways. He did inspire me by example, but it wasn't enough. I grew up woefully ignorant of the very things I admired so much in him. By the time I was old enough to do them myself, I had found other things which were very poor substitutes indeed for what I might have learned had my young hands been trained.

The guns Grandpa made were sought after from hunters far and wide. In his early years he depended on wild game to feed his large family. A lack of money called out the inventive creativity in him. He fashioned every part of the rifles he built, including the firing mechanisms and safety catches. Before gun butts were cushioned against kickback, he designed buffers out of cloth strips.

But Grandpa was not all business. He crafted a revolver which fired when a penny was inserted into it. Mother had conniptions over that, relating dire accounts of those who had been killed by playing with guns. She forbade me even to carve guns out of wood. Playing cowboys and Indians was out of the question. All of her objections, of course, were no competition for a grandfather whom I idolized as a gunslinger, if he was only so in my boyish fantasy.

One morning in early spring of '55, my uncle Roy announced that Grandpa had lost his driver's license. He had just turned eighty and it had been removed from him to prevent him from becoming a menace on the road. This was a terrible piece of news, since Grandpa gave us rides on crucial occasions, like going to the circus at the fairgrounds north of town. Uncle Roy was philosophizing about the arbitrary nature of the government's decision to yank Grandpa's license. I think he thought he'd have to ferry him around and the idea kind of riled him.

"So what are they going to do next, yank his teeth if he doesn't chew just right? Maybe the inspector who tested him has bad eyesight and marked the test wrong."

Uncle Roy was being shushed by my aunt Wilma, who hated controversy worse than I hated boiled pork hocks.

"Carrying on about Grandpa's license isn't going to get it back for him," she chided. "You'd think by the way you're talking it was you who lost out. You're more worked up than he is."

Uncle Roy scowled and mumbled something about laws being for criminals, not nearsighted citizens.

My thoughts turned to Grandpa. Cutting across the field behind our house on my way to his place, I imagined how sad he must be, having been deprived of his driving pleasure. My idol had been grounded by the bureaucrats.

Rushing into the porch, I slammed the screen porch behind me, "Grandpa, Grandpa!" I called.

No answer. All was quiet in the house. Then I heard a drill cutting into steel. I jumped the stairs, still running, and saw Grandpa bent over a pair of bicycle frames. "Grandpa," I grabbed his arm, "Mommy says you can't drive anymore."

He looked at me with twinkling blue eyes, "No, I lost my license but they didn't say I couldn't drive."

"What are you going to do?"

"It's still OK to ride bicycles, son. Motorized bicycle cars are not forbidden because there are none. That's why I'm building this."

Slowly, a vehicle which had no bureaucratic transportation category emerged out of my Grandpa's fertile brain and his innovative hands. No whimpering requiem for lost privileges. No bitter diatribe against lobotomized politicians. Just the quiet brilliance of a man who would not cut his losses and head for home. Putting his mind to work, he found solutions to his setbacks, rerouted plans and accepted adversity as part of life. I have used his example to great advantage several times and found that things I thought impossible were not insurmountable when I pushed through.

The double motorized bicycle machine was a beaut. Two bicycle frames paralleled one another, three feet apart, joined by a framework upon which rested a padded seat and floor-board moving up into a firewall. It was like a low-slung stage-coach. Balloon tires offered a smooth ride. A handy carrying cage was located behind the seat. The two bicycle handle bars had become one, streamlined so that the front wheels moved in unison. To my delight, a bell and horn adorned the steering mechanism. Artistically decorated, the machine graced the streets of Steinbach and the highways beyond, moving safely along and incredibly free of license fees. Grandpa had turned lemons into lemonade.

Grandpa got older, as grandpas do. He got older much quicker after Grandma died. He spent less time in his work-shop, more time on his bench in the garden. The super double motorized bicycle machine didn't leave the yard as often.

One day they took Grandpa to the hospital with pneumonia and a weakened heart. He got the hiccups two days later and a week afterward he died.

I went to his shop. It was quiet. Some unfinished work lay on the bench. He had left a few things incomplete, but not much. I can still see his hands today if I try, guiding a hand plane across a pine plank or tapping an etching tool for hours to produce the head of a majestic stag on a silver-plated gunstock. Busy hands, excellent hands, committed hands, creative hands.

When God asked Moses, "What is that in your hands?" Moses said it was just a shepherd's staff. In God's hands it became much more.

If you give Him your hands and whatever they hold, you will leave behind much to others when He calls you home.

5 Someone Saved My Life Tonight

The night I set about to take my own life was an experience of faith. How could I possibly describe escape from teenage suicide as an act of faith? The Bible says, "Faith is the substance of things hoped for, the evidence of things not seen" (Hebrews 11:1, KJV). On the night of this story, what was eternal crossed time and space to reveal itself to the senses of a desperate boy. There *was* evidence of things unseen.

How much faith did it take for Jesus to still the raging storm on the Sea of Galilee? Little, apparently, since He said to the disciples, "O ye of little faith" as they cried out to Him, "Master, master, we perish" (Luke 8:24, KJV).

I'll tell you how much faith it took—enough faith to wake Jesus. My heart was crying out in rebellion and despair, "Master, I perish," the words of my pain spoken in a silent scream. I was not asking for His help; I was past that place. But God doesn't wait every time for our words to be spoken. He sees the invisible, hears the inaudible and does the impossible. He has a Father-heart.

I was a rebellious teen. Rebellion is the act of replacing God with yourself; it factors the presence of God out of life's equation. Sometimes it brings down a devilish darkness which will swallow the rebel in an instant and leave him groping for the light. Contrary to appearance, rebels are easily led—led into blind alleyways of anger and confusion. All rebels sell out to power—dark and seductive promises spoken in deceit to their gullible hearts.

The promise I heard in my young life was this: "Don't let anyone control you, and you will know the delicious taste of freedom. Control is slavery; boundaries are restrictions. God is a boring, joyless tyrant." I believed it for a good long while.

Satan, the adversary of Christ and all who follow Him, is an ancient, clever foe. Human intelligence is no match for him. Only God's wisdom and discernment can protect us from his wiles. When Jesus overcame death He defeated Satan on our behalf. We no longer need to fear death if we trust in Christ. When Jesus rose in power He held up the demonic realm to shame and divested it of power to overcome those who believe in Him.

But Satan is causing as much havoc as he can, lying about God, about ourselves and about himself. He is the father of lies. All we have to do to be deceived by him is to ignore the truth. Jesus said, "I am the way and the truth and the life. No one comes to the Father except through me" (John 14:6).

Satan loathes the eternal life offered freely by Jesus. He hates God's love and mercy, twists His words and blinds the eyes of any who believe in Christ. He was leading me, at the age of fifteen, blindfolded to the brink of death—desperate, defeated and in despair.

I had always suspected there was more to God than the religions I saw around me. There was a restless longing deep within me which roamed the dark chaos of my thoughts. Now and then, like a firefly in the night, a flash of light broke the darkness, revealing a loving God. Glimpsed ever so momentarily, it sent a signal, "I'm here, I'm here, I'm here."

My grandmother, who knew of my reckless behavior, offered up her love to me with hugs and home-cooked food. Her penetrating Russian blue eyes would find my own and twinkle in uncompromised love. "You're a good boy," she insisted. "Leave good tracks for others to follow."

Her presence was a haven from the hate I had harbored for almost a decade by 1959.

Somehow, entering her humble two-room cottage was like stepping into a demilitarized zone. Along with the pervading smell of liniment, the fragrance of love was everywhere. It diluted my disillusionment and neutralized my anger. She seemed to owe me nothing and offer me everything.

Her gentle hands, misshapen with arthritis, would rest upon my shoulders as I gobbled down what she set before me. Sometimes she would tuck a couple of her few dollars into my shirt pocket, saying that she had found extra that week.

I wanted to cry in her ample bosom, to pour out the bitter brew of my fermented sadness. I never found the freedom to do that. But the clear outline of her unconditional love, uncluttered by many words, kept me from wandering too far, kept me from going over the edge into the place of no return.

Sitting and knitting in her wicker rocker beside the space heater, she would tell me about my father. "Your father was a kind and gentle man," she reflected, not looking up. "Always had time to visit and help me with my garden. He often brought me wild roses from the gravel pits. He would pick them with his bare hands. His hands were hard but his heart was soft, like yours."

I wanted her to stop talking. The lump in my throat was choking me. But this wise woman was allowing me to compare myself to my father without addressing my personal guilt. She awakened my memories, melting the hardness of pain away. Where no rebuke could have reached me, her careful compassion walked like the risen Christ, through my walls of fearful isolation.

Most of my time was spent away from harbors such as Grandma's place, out on the rolling sea of rebellion, and Jesus was asleep in my boat. I had less faith than the disciples: I did not cry out or wake Him. Inside and out I carried responsibility for my family's survival, as a young boy and into young manhood. It was not that mother did not work. She did—like two men sometimes. Nor was I deprived of food, clothing or shelter. The bare essentials were mine. And much love, which my blindness kept me from recognizing.

Past these, where the soul lives, I occupied the lonely and unpredictable expanses of weeks, months and years without a purpose beyond survival. Life was burdensome, restrictive and disruptive. It grew increasingly dispensable for me. In all fairness to friends and family, many reached out to help me in my rebellion, some to bless and some to blame. In the deepening twilight of what I now recognize as depression, the two merged and became the same.

Why was I locked up this way? My heart had decided that someone, almost everyone, had to repay me for my losses. Total strangers were assigned prices for my misery: destruction of their property, random words of cursing, even mockery of those who were different than I. Isolation became my security and at the same time my prison. Life was utterly routine and arduous at a time when my whole being craved excitement. Work supplanted opportunities for pleasure.

In her insecurity, my mother tried to select my friends and restrict my associations so she could keep me near her.

There was a lot of guilt imparted when I broke these boundaries. She was needy and so was I.

One spring when I was twelve, a teenage boy molested me. The confusion and rage which emerged with me into late adolescence was profound. I did not understand it then; I do now. It is only God's preserving grace which prevented me from killing someone. I used my words like a sword to cover up my sadness and anger during this time of my life. I would fantasize the murder of those who made my life difficult.

I was simply not who I had been. I had changed. My father's grave was the lightning rod of my grief during the storms of adolescence. His marker read, "Resting where no shadows fall." How I wanted his shadow to fall on me and my restless soul! It did not happen there.

Sometimes when I visited, crouching beside the stone, I spoke to him as if he had not left. Our conversations were the soliloquy of a broken heart. They are echoes of Gethsemane. "If it is possible, Father, let this cup pass from me. Who am I? What shall I do? Who were you? Why are these things happening to me? Am I going to be OK?"

There were far more tears than words as the wind came and went in the tops of the orderly fir trees around the cemetery. There were many questions and no answers.

"I'll do my best," I promised him. "I'll take care of everything at home."

And so I tried, but my demons raged on unfettered, and my promise went forgotten. Memories of my absent father were no match for my present realities.

At fifteen, one night in early March, I could find no comfort, not even at my father's grave. Schoolwork was left untouched. My brother Chris, five years younger, on whom I doted, grew puzzled by the disappearance of my usual camaraderie. "What's wrong?" he asked.

"Nothing," I lied.

The truth was that I was thinking suicide. My heart and mind had become a black hole of despair. There were not enough stars in the darkness, too many years left to live. In the naivete of youth, I could see no escape from life's road, disappearing ahead of me into a desert.

The afternoon of the night I've mentioned found me walking home with Bob, a friend also fatherless and angry. There was a trilogy of us; Andy was the third. Bob and I emerged from our fatherless youth restored in our later years. The journey took its toll on us and those around us, but I believe that the prayers of friends and family made the difference.

Side by side we walked, the three of us heading home in the waning afternoon sun. Fatherless, latchkey children who had lost the key to our lives.

"What are you doing tomorrow night?" Andy asked of no one in particular.

"Going to the rink," Bob answered. "There's a game on. Everyone's going to be there."

"Like who? Margo probably."

I hated it when they talked about girls. I would not have dreamed of speaking of a special girlfriend at fifteen. In my world there was no room for girlfriends. Andy shoved Bob into a snowbank and they fought like young bulls. Nothing was ever decided.

"What would Margo want with a bozo like you?" Andy howled. "You know, Randy is going to pick her up in his dad's car tonight. She's not going to want to hang around town with you!"

We laughed but we knew the bold truth. Our poverty was our perimeter, the border of our isolation. I had even more borders around me. Heaving and puffing, Andy and Bob caught up to me. "What are you doing tomorrow night?"

Like a shooting star from out of nowhere, burning up in the atmosphere of my anger my answer came, "I'm going to kill myself."

"You're nuts! You don't mean that!"

"Yes, I do."

My lack of intensity surprised me. I almost felt peaceful, as if my turmoil was over as the words left my mouth. There was a long silence as we trudged on side by side.

Bob spoke first, "If you do, you'll go to hell."

I had long since decided I was already in hell. "I don't care. Anything is better than this."

A pall of awkward quietness hung over us until we reached the place where we parted ways. They went one direction and I the other. I remember not wanting to go home.

As I walked on alone it seemed as if an evil presence filled me. My heart felt like stone! I had crossed beyond the boundaries I usually transgressed. As usual, mother asked me why I was late and where I had been.

"None of your business," I replied, using an expletive. She turned white, so extraordinary was my response. My brother ran from the room covering his ears as I began to shout, screaming at her in a convulsion of blind rage.

"I won't be your slave anymore. You and your church can go to hell. Dad probably died to get out of here. I wish I were dead."

Mother was now sobbing in brokenness. She lay on the kitchen floor begging God to help her and to forgive me.

Standing over her, I laughed in a voice not my own. With an icy stare I spoke, "This is it for me. I hope you're satisfied!"

I turned and left. Her cries faded as I walked into the night towards the milling tower behind the lumberyard.

It was biting cold, but I felt nothing. In fact, my face felt hot. Ascending the wooden stairs of the tower, my mind repeated, "If you do, you'll go to hell. Your father is in heaven. If you do, you'll go to hell. Your father is in heaven."

Soon I stood on a platform high above the ground surrounded by a low railing. The only barrier between me and the ground below, between the ground and my tortured soul.

Jump to freedom, desperate thoughts thundered inside my head. *You have nothing to lose. Your pain will disappear. Hell will be over for you. Peace at last. It will only hurt for a second, and you'll sleep after that.*

Like a solitary soldier before the firing squad, I waited . . . for what, I do not know. Then I felt something which seemed to come from outside but was inside, deep inside—an arm resting across my shoulders. I could sense the weight of it and its protection all at once. Surprised but not startled, I wanted to turn but couldn't. My recollection is that an aching left my body and a comfort washed over me. Something was taken and something was given. The sensation was of my father's arm resting on my tired body beside him, sleeping on the truck seat going home from work.

The feeling left as gently as it had come. I stood there looking at the lights of the town for a long while. Something had released inside of me. The crushing weight I had felt was gone. I blew a circle of steam into the night and watched it float away. I felt distinctly lighter as I took the steps two at a time to the ground below. I wanted to go home. The days following seemed anchored to that visitation between heaven and earth. I can't explain what happened. I believe that someone saved my life that night.

My life of frustration and limitation continued. Mom and I patched things up. Two years later, I left home, spending many days and nights alone, living and working in strange places. But I never felt completely alone again. A guiding light had been set in the window of my soul. I followed it till it brought me home to the Father-heart of God.

6　The Anteroom

Dark, stormy nights have been doorways of
change in my life—outer and inner storms.
The night I nearly jumped from the mill tower into
eternity was such a night. It was also the very beginning of
another life for me. That night I entered another
dimension of realization. Something deep inside me had
taken a turn for home . . . the home of my heart. It put my
mind in touch with the consciousness that someone
spiritual was seeking me, drawing near to me. I believe it
was the Father God.

It was a landmark I could refer back to, get my bearings
by, in the years of my young wanderings. Like the dim recognition of the outline of someone approaching me as I

looked toward my horizons. At any rate, the future did not appear as empty as it had before.

This is not to say that my ways were less empty or more hopeful. My anger had not diminished by much, nor were my ways less rebellious; but something had inserted itself into my boiling emotions, something which took the edge off my bitter spirit. Something or someone tender and re-assuring. There seemed to be an awareness in me that no matter how confused or chaotic life became, my feet in their sinking would find solid rock. If you had asked me for an explanation beyond that, I would have likely shrugged my shoulders and walked away.

There were also practical indicators of change. I listened to other people a little longer than I would have before and more carefully. My own words, I think, were less abrasive and Mother, bless her heart, got more help from her irre-sponsible son. However, Mother's emotions remained raw until I left home a year or so later. Maybe numb would de-scribe it better than raw. When I cursed her and left to take my life I had spoken into being something irrevocable.

A bond between us had been torn apart by my rage. Like a hurricane ripping up deeply rooted trees, my accu-mulated anger had uttered words so destructive that mere passage of time could not heal them. We talked of course; we cried, and I said how sorry I was. All was forgiven, but a boundary had been crossed. The little boy who had lis-tened to her heartaches, her ever-present companion dur-ing her frequent visits to church, friends, relatives, the singer of comforting songs to her on Sunday afternoons, was no more. He had disappeared around the corner of the life he chose. And it was very different than hers.

In his place was a man-child intent on escaping his social and religious isolation, a fighter and a "fleer" rolled into one. It was a time to get back all I had given away and all that had been taken from me. My decisions would be my own from now on. The landlords of religion would receive no "rent" from me for the drab tenements they wanted me to live in. I would live in my self-created palaces of pleasure. I felt sure I would find peace there.

Death took my father, desertion took my mother. *I* deserted her. The life she represented was unacceptable to me so I left her soul and I left her presence. I lived in her home, but my life was elsewhere. She tried to keep our relationship alive, to keep with her what she sensed was slipping away. I would have none of it. The harder she tried, the more dramatic became my rejection of what she valued. The more strongly she persuaded me to follow, the further I lagged behind.

Chris, my brother, fun-loving, good-natured and sensitive, was lost in the turbulent wake of my daily conflicts with Mother. He floundered in the darkness of Mother's fear as she focused on me and my desperate struggles to extract myself from what I saw as the trap of my life.

Most of my time was spent away from home, at the pool hall or my friend Marty's house. Together we spent hours listening to Hank Williams or new, emerging rock stars like Elvis. When he arrived to change the music scene forever, we couldn't get enough of him. We emulated his dress, his hair, even his sneer.

Most of all we believed his musical message. The generation gap was valid; older people were irrelevant. We would go it on our own and our ideas were better than theirs. The great splitting edge of an axe had descended on society, forever dividing wisdom from ignorance. We believed and were deceived. Elvis became our messiah.

We spent hours in Marty's bedroom. My bedroom was stark, with only Mother's pictures on my walls, but Marty's was adorned with posters of rock idols and Hollywood stars. He came and went as he pleased. His father, quite old by now, lived his own life as a mechanic.

Marty said he had never talked with his father about anything other than cars—and that only a little. His mom saw to the house and the physical needs of her family. She was constantly prevailing on Marty to eat better, sleep more and attend church with her. Ours was a bonding of rebellion. We were like two prisoners in the same cell, joined by confinement. It was us against the wardens.

One evening we were ensconced in Marty's bedroom working our way through his record collection. Occasionally we jumped to our feet from lying stretched out on the floor to jive to Chuck Berry or Elvis. We were grooving one minute and discussing the mysteries of life the next.

"What's your dad like?" I asked him one Sunday afternoon, to the background of "In the Ghetto" by Elvis.

He was silent for a long while. Finally, he answered, "Oh, he's like everyone else's old man, I guess." His com-

ments were more snorted than spoken, a cynical disposal of
his father into the vat of fatherhood.

Marty looked into the mirror fastened to the inside of his
bedroom door, running his comb through slicked-back
black hair. "What kind of a dumb question is that?" Then,
"What's yours—" He checked himself, awkwardly hesitated and then asked. "What was yours like?"

"I asked you first, besides I can hardly remember what
mine was like," I lied. The record played, "A young boy
dies and a mother cries in the ghetto." We fell silent, our
thoughts parallel but undisclosed in our boyish minds.

Marty spoke first, "My dad is a mystery," he said, staring blankly at the wall behind me. His choice of terms intrigued me.

"Oh yeah?"

"Yeah. He doesn't talk to me unless he wants me to do
something or I've done something wrong. He's Mr. Mystery," he said, waxing poetic. "Mom tries to get him to talk
at the table. Asks him about his day. He says, 'OK.' She
used to ask him about a lot of stuff—the cars he worked
on, his customers, just about anything. But he doesn't say
more than he has to. Then he takes off when he's finished
eating. Seems like he can't wait to get away from us."

"Your Mom must be ticked off at him," I sympathized.

"She told me to respect him 'cause he loves us." Marty
got up again to comb his hair. "My dad spends his week-
ends mostly in the garage. He hates my music but I think
he's just trying to get away from Mom and me. He works
on his 1957 Chevy. Washes and rubs it down whether he

drove it during the week or not. Mom says he's married to it.

"Uncle Jack hangs out with him in the garage. They talk about stuff they did when they were young and crazy. I was in the backyard last Saturday when Mom and Dad were yelling at each other in the kitchen. I heard her call him a stranger and she said she was his prostitute. Then he slammed the door and went to the garage like he usually does. I felt like punching my dad. She followed him this time. She was crying. He was playing his classical music and she went in to turn it down.

"My mom watched him work on his car. She said, 'We used to dance to music like that and you used to touch me like you touch that car.'

"Dad didn't answer her at all so she went inside again and talked to my aunt on the phone for a long time. Anyway, I decided I'm not getting married, no way!" Marty declared.

"Me either," I affirmed. But my mind played pictures of memories in which my father and mother laughed, chasing one another in the backyard with pitchers of water in hand, collapsing with laughter after their rollicking on the garden swing . . . talking and holding hands till evening settled over them.

"So what would you ask your dad if you knew he would talk to you?" I pressed on.

"You're weird," Marty injected. "Where do you come up with all this stuff?" as he swung a pillow at my head. "You must be queer or something!"

I swung back at him, then sat back on the bed. "No, I mean it. What would you ask him?"

Marty flipped the record, lay back on his bed and looked at the ceiling. He said nothing for a long time. I noticed a tear leave the corner of his eye and reach the pillow. "I dunno. I don't think he'd answer if I did ask, I guess." More silence. Then, "Maybe I'd ask him if he loved me." His voice subsided to a bare whisper as if passing judgment on his own dream, as if to say without words that it was far too much to ask for, like crying out for water in the middle of the desert.

I filled the awkward silence with the issue pushing against the inside of my mind. "That is the weirdest, man. Your dad is alive and won't talk to you, mine is dead and I talk to him every week." There was a cruelty about my innocence. My comments must have hurt Marty deeply.

I continued, "My dad talked to me, Marty, about stuff I haven't heard about since he died."

"Like what?"

"You know, things about him and me." Marty was listening expectantly to what I would say next. There was a thirst in his eyes. This was high adventure to his soul. "He said we were a team. He told me I would be a good and great man . . . that I could be whatever my heart said I should be. He asked me what I liked and why I liked it. He asked me why I was happy or sad. He even talked to me about God, but not the way they do at church. He said he loved me because I was his son and . . ." I couldn't keep on. Marty's eyes were riveted to me as if we were talking about sex. Suddenly the pain in my center rose up like a wounded beast charging into the circle of my sacred thoughts.

"But he's dead, Marty. Forever. It's just me now, alone with my mother and my brother!" I cursed profanely, catapulting myself into the face of my pain, flailing at the demons who mocked my losses. I had to give myself some sane reason for my father and me to be separated, but I couldn't. A hurricane hits out of nowhere; a place is destroyed; the storm moves on. What are the reasons for that?

Marty had only the mystery of a father who chose to observe him from a distance, dark and indistinct. I was ahead of him there. He seemed envious of me in a twisted sort of way. He puckered up his mouth, moving it from side to side, as he did when he felt awkward. He looked at me sprawled out on his beanbag chair and began, "I remember wanting my dad to talk to me. I used to hang around him in the garage, asking him to let me help. He let me do things. I'd throw out old tires, wash the floor, sort out nuts and bolts. But I wanted him to teach me about motors.

"So one day he said I should tighten one of the bolts on a customer's car . . . a real fussy customer. Well, I turned it too hard and I broke it off. It cost my dad big bucks to fix it too! He said I didn't have a knack for mechanics and it served him right for letting a boy do a man's job. He never let me help him after that." He spit into the wastepaper basket and continued.

"But I learned on my own at Sammy's place. Sammy's got a hot rod. He says he'll teach me about rods and broads. We pick up beer and chicks on Fridays. He lets me drive while he's in the back seat. Mom's always awake when I come in late, but Dad's asleep. Who needs him? He doesn't care and neither do I. Sammy is so cool!"

"Yeah, who needs them?" I echoed halfheartedly.

Now I wanted Marty to stop talking but he was on a roll. "Sammy says that's life for what it's worth. At least we don't have Reuben Barkwell's old man. He told me his dad took a belt to him. You should see the marks on his back! Said he nearly killed him. Probably drunk or something. Reuben said when he grew up he'd teach the old goat a few things. Says he can hardly wait to put him down. He actually said he'd like to kill him for the way he treats him and his mother."

I was saying nothing and Marty suddenly realized it. He rolled over, reaching for his bedside table. "Hey, you gotta see these pictures Sammy gave me," he chuckled, pulling some pictures of naked women from his drawer. "How would you like to love these?" he exulted. I glanced at the bedroom door, then stared transfixed by the pictures he held out towards me. We laughed lewdly, commenting to each other.

"Let's get out of here," I ventured later, "and see if Reuben's at the pool hall." Giving our hair one last comb, we pulled on our denim jackets and stepped out into the April evening. The mysteries we had probed unsuccessfully remained locked inside our young hearts—Marty's mystery, Reuben's rage and my pain. Why did Marty's dad ignore him and why, oh, why was mine gone? God had taken my

father and what kind of father would do that? Nothing
made sense except my pain.

I lit up a cigarette and offered one to Marty. He took it
and we walked along without talking. The moon was full
and shimmered off the water in the ditches beside us. We
began to walk faster. The quietness gave up too much
room to the thoughts we could not leave behind. When we
got to the pool hall Reuben was leaning against the wall
just outside the door.

"Hey, Rube," I said, walking up to him blowing smoke
into his face. He dragged deeply on the cigarette he was
smoking, then flicked the butt towards the curb, shrug-
ging his leather jacket into place as he stood up.

"You guys should've been here. Sammy dragged two
city guys with his '54 Ford, the one he stroked and bored
last week. The black marks are still over there where they
started. It was a killer! Sammy wiped the floor with those
slickers!"

Marty was not to be left behind. "We were looking at
girlie magazines. Makin' plans for the weekend. Sammy's
pickin' up beer and we're pickin' up chicks." Marty paused
to blow smoke rings.

I was the outsider. It seemed I was the outsider everywhere. Hank Williams sang inside my head, *I'm so lonesome
I could die.*

I looked at Reuben. His face was a mask, his mouth
straight and thin like a cut across his face, his eyes cold and
lifeless. Yet I liked Reuben, who had moved in from the
country a year earlier. There were brief moments during

which a funny, playful boy would emerge, but they were few. Mostly, he was brooding, always around the edge of things.

His father, Thomas Barkwell, was the opposite. Everybody seemed to know him. Bombastic, jocular, he never tired of telling whoever would listen how he had built his state-of-the-art farm with his own two hands. (My uncle Roy said it was hard to imagine how he could have done that given the hours he spent in the coffee shop.) Mrs. Barkwell was seldom seen around town. Thin, mousy, she looked worried all the time. Mother called her "that poor woman."

Slowly Reuben and I had become friends. He never spoke of life at home. It seemed to be a secret to be kept. Horses were his love, and he could draw them beautifully. It was the only time his face changed, softening into a look of something like love, and life would come into his eyes. The dark side of Reuben surfaced in phys ed class one afternoon. Mr. Patterson, our almost-retired teacher, was berating Reuben for his lazy manner. Mr. Patterson didn't like lethargic people, especially young ones.

He shouted into Reuben's face, "You move like an old plow horse! They move so slow they're hauled off to the glue factory! We don't want that happening to you, do we?" and with that Mr. Patterson grabbed Reuben's arms and forced them above his head until they touched. *"That's the way to do a jumping jack!"* he screamed. "When I say jump, I mean *jump!"*

What happened next immobilized the rest of us. Reuben was a big, muscled farm boy, and in a split second he seized his tormentor by the throat, flinging him to the ground. Only those near heard him utter a low growl of profanity into the face of Mr. Patterson, who stared up at him, agape with terror and humiliation. Slowly, Reuben lowered his cocked fist and straightened. Mr. Patterson scrambled to his feet, picked up his twisted glasses and smoothed his shirt, then ran inside. He returned with our principal and another teacher, and they led Reuben inside and beat him severely. We could hear the strap as it landed, but we never heard a sound from Reuben.

Many strokes later, it was over. Reuben was revered by the rest of us after that. There seemed to be so much power in his hate.

"My dad's coming," Reuben said, breaking into my thoughts. "Gotta go." The truck horn sounded repeatedly before it reached us standing at the curb in front of the pool hall.

"Been lookin' for you!" Mr. Barkwell hollered out the window. "Thought I'd find you here." He barely slowed the truck down to let Reuben leap onto the running board and scramble in. No hellos, no good-byes.

We watched the truck speed away. Through the rear window we saw Reuben duck a backhand from his father.

Marty and I said nothing as we turned to enter the pool hall. Then Marty cursed Thomas Barkwell.

Slowly summer edged out spring as 1960 unfolded. Faith and freedom remained locked in battle inside me—not that I understand either one, but I had my ideas. Faith was religion, and I didn't want it; freedom wasn't religion, and I did want that. Religion was a sniper. Scripture passages my mother had made me memorize would invade my thoughts at random, like bubbles of air rising to the surface of a pond. One quotation was "If the Son shall make you free, you shall be free indeed!" Another persistently nagged my quiet moments—"What a man sows, he will also reap. If you sow to the flesh, you will reap corruption. If you sow to the spirit, you will reap life everlasting."

In the gaps between sleep and slumber, I would wonder if somehow faith and religion were different. Religion made me sick, but there was something inside of it which was truthful and magnetic. I couldn't leave it alone. Something Jesus said—"If I be lifted up, I will draw all men to me"—pushed itself into my memory. There was nothing magnetic about religion that I could see.

Alone, confused, sad, angry, rebellious—that was me. Running away from something and to something else. What, I didn't know. Sleep was the best friend I had. Evenings got longer in front of the pool hall. Reuben showed up less as his hours at the farm took up his time. Marty went to the lake with his uncle. I wanted to hang out with Sammy, but he didn't take a shine to me.

One June evening I joined the usual bunch waiting for a table to open up. We stood outside waiting for things to happen.

Daniel, our church youth leader, walked up to me. He got right down to business. "Hi, Clint. Haven't seen you at church recently. Why don't you come this week. We've got fun times happening. How about it?"

"You've got to be joking," I laughed. "Why would I do that? The only way I'll go through those doors is in a coffin, and if that happens, I'll still be the most lively one in that joint!"

Wincing and red-faced, the youth leader left me standing, gloating at his embarrassment. It was a routine I enjoyed. I had become a prize fish to catch in a town increasingly concerned about its wayward youth. Sticking it to religious types was a way to make someone pay for the losses I inwardly attributed to God.

These people were afraid to live. I was afraid of no one, and my carefully cultivated reputation as a reckless rebel was growing. Fighting was a fascination to me. Any occasion would do to bait others into confrontation. Pouring out profanity, I would go into violent rages, earning a reputation as a crazy man. Mockery and blasphemy were at the tip of my tongue as my pain calcified, lying buried deep underneath my cavalier exterior.

My behavior came to the attention of the police. Occasionally they would pick me up for public disturbance and drop me off a block from home to save mother the embarrassment of gossiping neighbors.

There were two things which penetrated my stone-cold heart. One was a comment made one night as a member of the local constabulary dropped me off after a street fight.

"Your father would be hurt by what you're doing," he said. I said nothing in reply, but I felt it for days.

My grandmother told me that I was a fine boy, knowing full well the trouble I brewed around town. She insisted, as she fed me home-cooked meals, that God still loved me and she did too. I listened while she talked. She was my father's mother, after all.

In spite of these rare contacts with the truth about my life, I continued to build walls around my emotions which appeared unscalable. Coming in very late at night, I would hear my mother praying for me. It bothered me not in the least, and the day came when, for the sake of my mother's emotional health, I was asked to leave home. The final frontier had been crossed. I was now truly isolated. The seed of rebellion had matured. The harvest was ripe and it was surely a bumper crop.

In the spring of that year, my cousin Jeff, whom I admired as an athlete, had became the director of Red Rock Lake Bible Camp. "Why don't you come to work for me this summer?" he asked one day after stopping by the car wash where I worked.

"Doing what?" I inquired.

"Oh, hauling garbage, doing odd jobs around camp. That sort of thing."

I had recently acquired my driver's license and was excited about driving the camp truck, swimming, boating and other things to do. The presence of numerous teenage girls intrigued me as well. I agreed to go on one condition.

"What's that?" Jeff asked.

"I'll go if I don't have to attend chapel," I said.

Jeff was quiet for a bit, then agreed.

I think God chuckled when that conversation ended. I also have wondered what might have happened to me if Jeff had insisted on the camp staff rules. Did God give him a window through which he saw my broken heart and isolation?

Did Jeff sense that my father-thirst would lead me to the well of God's presence? The truth is that God's father-heart is irresistible to a seeker such as I was. He holds such icy hearts in His hands until they melt in the warmth of His loving grasp.

Summer came and I went to camp. By the end of the first week I had grown restless in my rebellion. It became increasingly necessary to remain aloof from others in order not to hear them speak of the wonder they experienced in knowing Jesus Christ personally. I was openly skeptical of these summer camp converts. Every year, I maintained, they came home jumping for Jesus, and in a few short weeks they were dancing with the devil. There was no way I would be suckered into that emotional trap.

"Are you coming to chapel tonight?" a pretty, blond-haired girl named Frances asked me over breakfast one morning.

"Naw, that's not for me," I replied.

Ignoring my answer, she continued, "Pastor Mark is telling us all about his life as a fighter." Pastor Mark, a former boxer, was the camp speaker. He was OK for an adult, but I had avoided him like the plague. They all had an agenda of one sort or another. He was not like other pastors I knew, though. He laughed easily and listened carefully when the kids talked to him.

"I won't be there," I reaffirmed to Frances. "Say a prayer for me," I quipped and got up to go. However, something or someone began to stir inside me from that moment on and I began to debate with myself about whether or not I would go.

Can't hurt, I guess. It's not as if you're going to fall on your face in there and get converted. You like fighting and it won't be some long, boring sermon on sin or something like that. That was me talking.

Another voice joined in. *Don't kid yourself. First he'll tell you his story for five minutes, then he'll plead with you to "get saved" for the next half hour. He doesn't care about you, anyway. He's getting paid to do this. Besides, the guys at home will hear how you're back in church and you'll look like an idiot.* That was the snake talking.

Why do you think Pastor Mark believes and lives the way he does? Why do you think he began to follow Me? This meeting is a must for you. That was God talking.

So the debate continued. But shortly after 7 that evening, I slipped into the chapel and sat in the back bench.

In fact, the snake was wrong. Pastor Mark's story took up the entire evening, after which he simply asked if anyone would like to return to the heavenly Father as he had and as the prodigal son had so many years ago. "If you do return to the Father, you'll find Him waiting for you." It is likely that my hardened heart and determined will could have resisted anything else but that. God knows what will unlock the doors of human resistance.

"Those of you who want to return to your Father, come into the anteroom back here where I will explain what I mean in more detail and pray with you."

My stomach tightened and my head spun. The anteroom . . . to meet my Father. Could this be God circling me back to the beginning of my broken journey? Was this my father calling me? Was life with the heavenly Father different than religion? Was it like life had been with Dad? Was there really safety, warmth, comfort, laughter, and enough to live life with personal joy, peacefully?

My view of religion included none of these. I had no hunger pangs for what was served by those who offered religion to me, but I was ravenous at that moment for what I saw laid out before me on the table of God's Father-heart.

I thought again about the text Pastor Mark had taught from—Luke 15. The story of the prodigal son, which is actually better named the story of the waiting father. It was hunger that drew the prodigal son back home to his father. The stench of pigs did not drive him home, nor the discomfort of the filth, nor the embarrassment of the job. It wasn't the penury of the position or even the memories of father's house. That came later. It was gut-wrenching hunger lodged in the core of his bowels which brought him to his senses.

Blaise Pascal, the French philosopher and mathematician once said, "There is a [Father-]God-shaped vacuum in every being which only He can fill." There are thousands of motives which draw people to God. All of them are ultimately related to the hunger for relationship. A relationship made possible only through faith in Jesus Christ who said, "I am the way and the truth and the life. No one comes to the Father except through me" (John 14:6).

Was Jesus arrogant, deluded, crazy or truthful? All evidence, historical or experiential, points to the latter. But only the human heart can decide the matter conclusively by trusting in Him, by receiving Him personally.

I walked slowly and purposefully to the anteroom. There was no one else there except me and the Father. Kneeling, I put my head down on my arms and cried. It seemed my head rested on something soft. I sensed the smell of leather and I felt a strong hand on my shoulder.

To describe how I felt is easy after all these years. The words "loved," "forgiven," "peaceful" and "free" come to mind. To explain the process of moving from a place of darkness to the light is impossible. That, I suspect, is reserved for the heart of each one who opens up his arms to the embrace of the Father who says, "I will never leave you nor forsake you" (Joshua 1:5).

After a long while I rose to leave the anteroom. My hand closed on the Swiss army knife in my pocket. I felt the cross embossed on its red plastic trim. "I'm back, Father," I whispered, "I'm back."

7   **Beloved Enemy**

When I met my heavenly Father I somehow felt reconnected to my earthly one. It was a vague sense of returning to what I had lost as a child. I tried to tell Reuben what had happened to me. He didn't understand. It seemed that a bridge to faith in my heavenly Father had in some way been built by my own. Reuben was not so lucky. In fact, he could not have crossed that bridge at all; the word of the Father was synonymous with danger. His father had set his son afloat on the high seas of life without a compass or rudder. His chances of survival were slim indeed.

Reuben quit school in grade nine. His father said it was all the education he would need to work on the farm. He had become increasingly withdrawn for the better part of a year; almost reclusive and more and more cynical. We had become close friends, and I missed his thoughtful, caring presence. It seemed a good balance to my impulsive and brash ways. Their family had no phone and lived several miles out of town. Finally we lost touch.

Then one Saturday afternoon, I ran into him downtown. "Hey Rube," I exclaimed, "where you been? Haven't seen you for a month! Whatcha doin'?"

"Nothing much 'cept work," he mumbled, looking down at the sidewalk. I was shocked at how drawn he looked and how his hands were cut and calloused.

"Doin' some long hours baling straw, eh?" I ventured.

He didn't raise his eyes but nodded.

"Hey, why don't you come in next Saturday? We'll play some pool."

"Can't, won't be around."

"Where you goin'?"

He ignored my question. "Gotta go," he muttered and walked up the street. I didn't see Reuben again until his father died.

As young men, we seldom talked about our lives at home. Reuben didn't talk at all about his.

When I finally learned the truth about Reuben and his family, I decided to tell his story. He knew the scourge of family violence as none of his friends did. The signs of abuse and violence perpetuated against women and children or men should be read by all. The offenders should be exposed, brought to justice and helped themselves. Justice and forgiveness were both represented at the cross of Christ. None of us will be held guiltless for ignoring them.

Violence almost destroyed my friend Reuben. It destroyed his mother and scarred his life. It is the essential contradiction of fatherhood and the ultimate rejection of a child.

Thomas Barkwell was a raw-boned farmer whose body had outlasted his mind. Each day was lived in the reality of years past. The room he occupied in the locked ward of the district hospital was inhabited by his body alone. Since dementia had claimed his thoughts, his hospital bed had become his hay wagon, reaper and plow. His pajama cords tied to the bed rail were the reins of Gypsy, his beloved Clydesdale. Holding them in his gnarled hands, he called out to his invisible steed, filling his empty days with the substance of his useful but distant years. He called out to those who could not hear him, and he heard their answers.

"You've got to enter his space," Helen, the head nurse in the psych ward, instructed the orderlies. "When you want him to settle down, tell him Mabel's calling him for supper."

Mabel, Thomas's wife of fifty years, had died in the spring. The event had marked the beginning of Thomas' decline. He had given no outward indication of grief while they laid Mabel to rest in the Place of Flowers Cemetery just outside of town. Because he had served on the town council, many had attended the funeral, but few—perhaps no one—could say they really knew Thomas. Not even Mabel could say that.

It was rumored that he was a very difficult man to live with. Occasionally Mabel would be seen with bruises on her arms and face, but these were always explained away in one way or another. Many suspected that Thomas beat his wife, but not one found the courage to discover the truth and confront the oppressor. And so the poor woman lived her days in the silence of a creature hunted, with nowhere left to run. Her countenance was downcast and she uttered hardly a word when in the company of strangers together with her husband.

He, on the other hand, had an opinion on everything, loudly voicing it to all within earshot. One might wonder how such a man could be elected to a town council. But he was, and he would neither be the first nor last private tyrant to receive public applause. It was simple, really. He had a backslapping, coffee shop relationship with the men of his municipality. Since men voters outnumbered the women two to one, and since Thomas Barkwell saved his rage for those he could dominate in private, no one knew both Thomas Barkwells.

The demands and criticisms of public life, met with a smile in the office, were paid for privately, in the currency of suffering endured by his wife and son. The jovial, caring, negotiative man seen in town functions was sullen, sarcastic and violent at home. The rich diet of popularity he craved and got from those who curried his public favor was denied him when the needs of those at home arose. A king doth not a good servant make. Mabel and Ruben knew his dark side. They did not worship nor applaud him. Eventually they merely tried to avoid him.

And so when Mabel's thin and plainly dressed body was returned to the earth, never to see, feel or hear Thomas's rage again, he lost the repository of his abuse. Thereafter, driven by guilt and isolated by Mabel's absence, his mind could not support the weight of his tortured soul any longer. He withdrew from public life, speaking to no one, going nowhere. Insomnia held the doors open for night terrors to visit him. Slowly he entered a land inhabited only by himself. It remained for his closest neighbors to check on him occasionally.

One of them, Samuel Bender, was passing Thomas' house on a clear February afternoon. Seeing no smoke rising from the chimney, he investigated and found Thomas unconscious on the barn floor. His great Holstein bull, the best anywhere, Thomas had said, was a malevolent beast. It had seemed to have turned on him, crushing his head against the stall wall. Covered in blood, Thomas was rushed to the district hospital. Incredibly, he survived and returned home again.

Some time later, Samuel Bender came by to check on him again and found him trying to put a harness on the hand pump in the middle of the farmyard, entreating it to follow him to pasture.

Samuel offered to give Thomas a ride to his field using his own horses, in reality his 1941 Ford. He had driven Thomas Barkwell and his untethered thoughts into the district hospital to reap what he had not sown: tender care and merciful understanding.

Nurse Helen gently removed the pajama cords from Mr. Barkwell's tight grasp. "Mabel's got supper for you, Thomas. It's time to put up Gypsy. I'll take him to the barn while you eat."

The fantasy was the same each evening. She knew it well.

One of the oddities about Thomas which made his dementia somewhat easier to abide was his poetic bent. He was adept at rhyming on the spur of the moment, concocting the wildest ditties as he sojourned in his days of mystery. At Nurse Helen's supper announcement, he intoned enthusiastically,

> Heave ho, home we go
> Mother Mabel's calling.
> Clip clop, don't you stop!
> Soon the night is falling.

Helen sagged against the bed, tears of laughter starting down her cheeks. "Where do you get that stuff, Thomas?"

She pried loose the pillow he was straddling in the absence of a tractor seat. "Time to eat, Thomas," she repeated. "Tonight the carolers are coming. Do you want to sing?"

> Sing a song of six pence
> Pockets full of rye

Four and twenty bottles
Now I'll drink 'em dry.

It was her signal to leave. He would remain alone again. Not one visitor had come to see him since he had been admitted. No one had touched him, spoken to him or listened to him who had not been paid to do so. He still cried out in the night and had to be restrained from hurting himself. His eyes would be red and fury-filled as he screamed at unseen beings. "Get away from me, scum of hell," he would cry out, shielding himself with his arms from the phantom entities. "Don't let them take me. Call Reuben, call Reuben, call Reuben."

An injection was all the solace they had to give him, and he would sink like a tranquilized beast into the unfeeling arms of a dreamless sleep. Sleep without rest; for as Isaiah the prophet wrote, "The wicked are like the tossing sea, which cannot rest, casting up mire and mud. 'There is no peace,' says my God, 'for the wicked' " (Isaiah 57:20).

Helen had read Thomas' short medical file. His son Reuben was mentioned but there was no known address of his whereabouts. Mr. Barkwell's lawyer said he thought he lived in Las Vegas. Now at her nursing station, she prayed silently in the deliberate manner of one who believes she is being heard.

"Heavenly Father, you know and see all things. All power is in your hands. Your word says that Jesus died for Thomas and Reuben and was resurrected from the dead to set them free from hate and fear and to forgive them. Heal their broken hearts, Lord. Have mercy on them. I know that you can do what no man can do. I pray these things in Jesus' name."

She had never yet prayed with a patient, but she had prayed for them all. In the manner of one born to care for others, her prayers were the completion of the loving works of her hands. Her life was devoted primarily to nursing, which she also considered to be her life's calling and purpose. Her relationship with the God she knew permeated all else in her life. Her religious words were few and well chosen. Her love was impartially and generously given.

That night Thomas slept free of night terrors. Helen checked on him one last time. Looking at his craggy face in the dim light, she wondered how a son could abandon his aging father to allow him to stumble madly into the darkness of a lonely death. A flush of anger came on the heels of her thought. "If I knew where he was, I'd phone him and give him a piece of my mind. I wonder where he is?" she murmured.

The answer to her question sat at an all-night bar underneath the bright lights of Las Vegas . . . the city of dancing girls, money changers and those who cannot sleep. Thomas' son was one with the city which steals the souls of the lonely. There he gambled with his life, devalued by a fatherless heart.

Reuben had lived in a crucible of tyranny, driven by secret demons. Thomas Barkwell had had a relationship with his son which alternated between brooding silence and unexplainable rages.

Walking a tightrope of potential rejection, Reuben had lived in abject fear of failing. His crushed and broken spirit bore testimony to the reality of how frequently he had failed to cross the chasm of his father's wrath successfully.

Like the time, as a boy, when his foot had slipped on a patch of ice, sending several dozen eggs soaring to land on him and the barn floor. Falling with a cracking jolt on the frozen surface, he bit his tongue, crying out in pain. It was nothing compared to the lash of his father's words which landed fast and furious on his young ears. "Can't I trust you with anything? How often have I told you to watch your step? Are you blind and lame? You little klutz. Why do I send a boy to do a man's job?"

Why indeed! The revelation passed unobserved by Thomas' oblivious soul. That his son was much too young and untaught, too slight and afraid of error to meet his expectations had not entered his mind. So he pursued his unseen rage, purple-faced like a ceremonial mask.

"You'd think you could do one thing right by now. Here, give me that."

He grabbed the pail and in so doing spilled some eggs himself. His own awkwardness exposed, he redoubled the scorn raining down upon Reuben. "Get out of here, you useless twit. Go help your mommy wash dishes. Maybe you can do that right. God knows you're not a farmer. You're a waste of my time." Reuben didn't move to leave. It was like playing dead at the feet of a grizzly bear. He had his arms raised to soften the now inevitable blows. Thomas loomed over the helpless child. Uncontrollably, he dupli-

cated the sin of his own father. His son lay bound like a sac-
rificial lamb before him on the altar of his pain.

Reuben's upraised arm was a futile gesture as Barkwell's
huge boot crashed into the boy's frail frame, lifting him off
the ground and throwing him into the filthy barn gutter.
Reuben's eyes were wide with terror, fixed upon the one
beneath whose pain he lay buried. He could not draw his
breath. Manure soiled his contorted face.

"I've had enough of you and your clumsy daydreaming,
you little rebel."

Lifting him by the neck, Thomas carried him gasping to
the feed storage room. There he threw his son into the
darkness and the confusing peace of a fatherless place. The
door was slammed in undiminished anger followed by the
sound of a swivel lock and the receding bootsteps of the
tormentor.

Not daring to cry out, Reuben sobbed softly, wrapping
his arms around himself; rocking his aching body. He felt a
nausea pass over him and a sense of free-falling into darkness. "What have I done?" he murmured through swollen
lips. "What have I done?"

It was a question no one could or would ever answer for
him. It was asked on and on throughout his years. Every
time the circumstances of life and the choices of others
would leave him confused and hurting in darkness, the
question would come again. Now he waited in the barn
until his mother came, much later, to cradle him, clean and
comfort him in ways his father would not notice. Time

moved him along, unhealed and increasingly divested of any hope for a father's love.

He grew strong and handsome but inside he grew not at all. He watched his father caress the face of Gypsy, the beloved horse. Gypsy lived by instinct and never made mistakes. The great horse without a will of its own had become the recipient of Thomas Barkwell's kind words, gifts of sugar and tender touch. Gypsy, whose will had been broken and absorbed by Thomas'.

Ruben remained untouched, and he grew bent-backed by labor unsuitable for a boy of growing years. His heart became a windswept glacier, crossed only by an occasional explorer challenged by its cold surface. It took years for his longings for a father's love to die.

Sometimes, returning to the house from his farm chores, he would stop outside to look into the warmly lit windows. Standing alone under a starlit sky, he gazed unnoticed at his father reading the paper at the kitchen table. More than once he caught himself with his hand in midair as he feigned the touching of his father's face. And he did more than that in his fantasy. He did what no man would have dared to do. He kissed his father's leathered face.

He longed for what no one should have to long for—to not be himself, to be someone else, someone his father might love. Occasionally melting into grief, he would turn and flee back into the company of four-footed beasts, to lie with his head upon the horse his father loved. There in the sanctuary of a barn, questions of God presented themselves to him, questions he had heard others ask, "My God, my

Father, why have you forsaken me? If it be possible, let this cup pass from me."

And always the silence would answer him, but sometimes a dove would coo and usually the mercy of sleep descended to dissolve his despair. His longings turned to lustfulness. The touch his heart yearned for was found in the companionship of women equally unloved.

A burning brand had sizzled on the raw flesh of his soul. Withdrawn, it clearly read, "I am unworthy of my father's love. However long I wait in my pain, he will never come for me. Even a mother's love cannot protect me from my father's power. Power is stronger than love. If I don't love myself, no one will."

One night, in fact on his seventeenth birthday, he hopped the midnight bus to Las Vegas. There he wielded the power of lust, leaving in the dark many longing women. There he loved money until it owned him. He built a life moated from his past, walled by hidden hate and guarded by the sentinels of brokenness.

Time passed. Then came this night, a night like no other before it, for Reuben and Thomas, his father. What made this night different? What was it that finally spanned the distance between their hearts? What voice was loud enough to calm a tormented man into a peaceful sleep and waken a son from a deep and dreadful slumber?

To the skeptic, it was a Las Vegas deal, a roll of the dice. To the believer, it was the faithful prayer of a country nurse. We may never know; we certainly don't understand. It may not require an explanation.

In Las Vegas, Reuben left a glass of whiskey at the bar, excusing himself from the woman who had caught his fancy for the evening. For the first time in years, he sat before his fireplace, thinking about his father. For the first time in his memory, he wanted to see his face. A feeling rose up inside of him that surprised and perplexed him. It was a mixture of longing and hate, pain and pity.

His father, his beloved enemy, had for disturbing reasons reentered his thoughts after decades of absence. But it was unmistakable. He had returned along with the memories. A kaleidoscope of shifting chaos, new patterns of pain revealed themselves with each turn of recall. There was no gate for Reuben's tears, but a sweat rose off his soul and beaded his forehead. He noticed himself rolling the newspaper he held tightly with clammy hands. Suddenly he reared like a wounded animal, flinging the paper into the fire. "Burn in hell, old man."

Grabbing the poker, he stabbed at the paper curling in the blaze. As he did so, the obituary page fell open and the faces of strangers stared back at him. Mostly old fathers soon to disappear, ashes to ashes.

He loathed the impressions being made upon his calloused soul. It had all been settled in his own mind: His father's death was to be a formality. Long since, he had planned to have his father cremated by the executor of Thomas' will, who was to forward estate proceeds to Reuben. He wanted his inheritance. It was all he wanted from his father. Let those gather who might; he would not attend the exit from life of the man who had never entered his own. After one more drink he headed for bed.

A sleeping pill failed to bring him rest. He rose again and fixed himself a drink. Wandering into the den, he picked up the TV remote. Not in the mood for sports or comedians, he surfed the channels. Suddenly a white-haired man looked at him from the screen. It was as if he had entered the room where Reuben sat. His still, clear blue eyes carried a welcome Reuben had never felt before. Then he spoke, "You may be far from home tonight, a fugitive from your past. Your life may be full of pleasure but empty of love. Are there six men who love you in your life who would come to carry you to your final resting place if you died tonight?"

Reuben's mouth was dry. He sipped on his rum and Coke. "You need the love of others, other men. More than this, you need the love of your father, the love your heavenly Father wants to give you."

Reuben pressed the remote and landed on a sports channel but within seconds he was back, and the white-haired man continued. "Everything your lonely heart has longed for begins with a cry for help. Only God can break the chains that have imprisoned you inside your empty life. You need help to forgive and be forgiven, to receive His love and give it away. Tonight's your night to start over. He's there with you now. Listen and He'll speak to you."

The remote clicked off, but it was too late. A window to his soul had opened, and the light had entered. An earthquake, with his soul as its epicenter, shook him where he

sat. His trembling body gave silent testimony of a deep re-
alignment in progress. The stone blocking the door of his
grave was about to move to make room for life within him.

It seemed as if warm hands held his frozen heart and it
began to melt. The drops slid down his cheeks; they became tributaries and then a river. A voice unlike any he had
ever heard spoke inaudible but unmistakable words to his
inner being. *I love you, Reuben. I always have, like no one else
can or ever will. I love your father too. My love for you is free and
unconditional. Your names are written on My hands. Your pains
were beaten into My back. I was forsaken for you so that you would
never be lonely in My love. Your sin and pain I wash away in the
blood of My Son, Jesus. I am your heavenly Father. Reuben, I
want you to take My love, and Reuben, I want yours too.*

The sadness which had entombed his fatherless heart
drained into the presence of the One who embraced him
there. Forgiveness fell on his fevered soul like cool rain. A
sense of indescribable love surrounded him and he had the
sense of being gently kissed—a kiss on the face of a run-
away returned home. He had touched his Father's face at
last.

"Thank you, Lord, for loving me," he sobbed into the
darkness. He thought of his earthly father. "Forgive me for
hating you, my father. I'm so sorry for all the wasted years.
I forgive you. Father, I forgive you."

The simplicity and intensity of his emotions, the radical
reversal of will, would be summarily discounted by the
skeptics, who would assign a psychological label to his experience and remain safely untouched by its power. But

Reuben rose in the morning, sane and in his right mind, to seek after integrity and walk a journey, the destination of which would become the city of joy.

At 8 a.m. the next morning, Nurse Helen answered her phone: "Hello."

"Hello, it's Reuben Barkwell, Thomas Barkwell's son. How is he doing?"

Helen sat stunned, going over her previous evening's conversation with God. "As well as can be expected, I guess, Reuben. We haven't spoken before, have we?"

"No." His speech was slow and reflective. "I haven't seen Father for years."

The weight of his confession hung unaddressed between them. Searching for an appropriate response, Helen went to the surface. "Where are you calling from?"

"Vegas. It's my home now."

Having decided on a course of protocol, Helen asked, "What can I do for you, Reuben?"

It was his turn to stammer, "I-I was wondering if I could speak to him. He's there, isn't he?"

Helen knew the moment of truth had arrived. "Uh, your father is in and out of reality, Reuben, mostly out right now."

Tears, for the second time in years, started to make their way down Reuben's face. "Would he know me if I came to see him?"

"Maybe. I encourage you to try."

She wanted to rail on him for having abandoned the old man but politely tried to gain a commitment instead. "When do you think you'll be coming?"

She was shocked by the direct sincerity of his answer. "I'll be on a plane tonight. I should be there tomorrow."

The practice of unforgiveness prevents us from receiving forgiveness. One must be poured out to make room for the other. It is not that God our Father is unwilling to forgive us. There is simply no room to receive and experience forgiveness while we are full of unforgiveness.

Forgiveness is not denying you have been wronged. Nor is it feeling OK about your offender. It is simply doing what Jesus did for you—canceling his behavioral debt. In releasing your offender from his debt, you are saying, "You no longer owe me for what you have done. Jesus has forgiven you and so do I. I may still feel hurt, sad, betrayed, but you will not have to pay for that in the way I treat you. I will not punish you for your behavior."

Forgiving someone may not mean that you trust him or that a monetary debt is necessarily erased, but it will mean that you will have an attitude of love even while justice is being done. The core question of forgiveness is this: Do I owe Jesus more than my offender owes me?

I still see Reuben. His father died some years after Reuben returned to honor him in the only way he could. Not denying the past, Reuben extended to his father the same mercy God had given him. Reuben released his father from relational debt. That is one half of forgiveness, the only half we are responsible for to those who have broken our lives.

Reuben Barkwell was freed from the consuming affliction of resentment. The warden of his prison was unforgiveness. Thomas Barkwell didn't deserve forgiveness . . . but then again, neither do we.

Reuben made room in his life to know the Father-heart of God. He drank the clear water of that relationship and there was enough left over for Thomas Barkwell as well.

Thomas never recovered their lost years. But Reuben did know the miracle of healing that comes to a broken heart when God's unconditional love takes the place of unforgiveness. Who knows? You may also sleep better at night, as he did.

8   Two Thirsty Sons

The discovery of my spiritual sonship, as releasing as it was, led to ever-deepening realizations of my own brokenness. I was anchored in God's love, but the seas of my past and present life continued to rage about me. I had run so far to get away from my pain that I had lost sight of who I was. I had rejected the young boy, the young man who felt so rejected, so alone, so hopeless, and I tried to become someone different. My spirit had been made whole. My mind, emotions and will were still trapped in a prison of my own choices . . . choices to set myself free rather than to be set free, to trust no one to guide my life, not even God, to control life and all that it involved so that never again would I be controlled by others in any way.

My heart had experienced the nearness of the Father-heart of God, but I would not let God be Lord as He is. He could be my Father, but I would be my lord. A good father, however, doesn't make those kinds of deals with the sons he loves, and God is the best Father there is.

So, out of the fear of losing I made sure I took care of myself. Winning, gaining, was all-important, however that had to be done.

My thirst for relationship was a great contradiction. I dared not get too close to anyone, since he (or she) was sure to disappear sooner or later. Years of poverty, not being with the "in" crowd, had convinced my soul that I wasn't attractive enough to be loved just the way I was, so I used charm, wit and athleticism to break into social circles. I believed it was not who I was, but what I could do that would gain for me the acceptance that I wanted.

My spirit had been made new by God but my soul remained broken. My Father in heaven, no doubt, waited longingly for me to love Him with my soul as well. He did not force me to do this. He did, however, allow me to experience ever-increasing thirst to know the fullness and freedom of His Father-heart. Today, looking back, I see portraits of two sons in the town I called home—myself and Simon Lafort. We were both different kinds of misfits. We were both drunk on different things.

You either laughed at Simon Lafort or pitied him, depending on the condition of your heart. I laughed at him a lot. We were both misfits in our town, but I was trying to fit in and he wasn't.

Simon did daily combat with the demon of alcohol. Well, maybe he didn't battle much—perhaps not at all. Everyone Simon's age looked old to me, but he was forty-five and looked more than old. He looked worn out.

Simon lived on the outside of things. He watched TV through the large windows of Parson's Electric where Mr. Parson kept a TV on all night for advertising purposes—so Mr. Parson's son, my friend Blair, told me. On Saturday evening around 11 o'clock, Gorgeous George or Bulldog Bower or Gene Kiniski could be seen wrestling on the flickering screen.

One of my older memories is a picture of extraordinary pleasure. In it Simon is standing on the sidewalk outside Parson's Electric in the pouring rain, his Aussie hat pulled down low over his bald head, his collar turned up. The street light reflects off his leathery face, making it appear clean and glistening in the rain. His lined face, which sagged into sadness, is transformed into uplifted delight as he toothlessly beams at the scenario before him.

His eyes are wide and bright, riveted to the drama inside on the black-and-white screen. Rocking on the balls of his feet, his hands are raised in front of him. Dodging, weaving at the waist, he feigns jabs and uppercuts, laughing in his whisky-worn voice, "Give it to him, Georgie Boy! Give it to him! Right on the kisser. Up she comes, down he goes."

I've wondered what it is in that memory that holds my fascination. Maybe it's the sheer incongruence found in the scene: The discomfort of the rain and the late-night loneliness over against the warmth of the light and the electronic people whom he addressed so freely, who did not know he was there and did not resent his presence. So, he danced and he ducked, one with the drama, out in the rain, feeling no pain.

Simon had a daily routine. It was as unusual as he was, but it was his routine. Only a few compassionate people saw to it. The last time I checked, there were no public plaques to applaud their kindness to Simon in propping up his life, but I am told there will come a day when what they did for him in secret will be openly rewarded.

Usually by 11 each morning, Simon had arrived at the local beer parlor. He would cut the grass and remove yesterday's garbage, burning it in a forty-five-gallon barrel drum. Bottles needed sorting and the floors sweeping. In winter, he kept the public sidewalk clean as a hound's tooth. How many sober pedestrians, I wonder, avoided bodily injury because Simon, not so steady on his feet, kept that sidewalk clean?

Having duly earned what he was about to consume, Simon was served beer approximately one per hour. Each weekday from 11-9 was thereby consumed. The only personal status Simon ever had was found in that place. At the tables in that sanctuary of manly exchanges, Simon, the head patron, talked. Outside he said nothing. Inside, holding forth on international politics or great philosophical issues, he divulged his thoughts. Words of a man gifted with original thinking, unique perceptions and deep understanding. But they grew increasingly garbled as the day wore on. Any astute observer would realize that Simon was a man of uncommon mind. The dark secrets of his soul had captivated him in a dungeon of isolation from which his jailer would temporarily release him each time he drank.

Drinking was prohibited in most homes in our town; religious people who drank usually did so clandestinely. The citizens would call him to account—saints and sinners alike reached out to him. Sometimes Simon was beset upon zealously and warned sternly of his foregone doom if he refused to comply. In utter frustration one evening, he exclaimed to someone intent on his conversion, "Everyone talks about how much I drink. No one talks about how thirsty I am!" There was little left to say.

What was the craving which had snared the soul of Simon, enlisting his body to share the pain inside of him? Why had he found his comfort in the empty promises of booze? What had obscured his view of a Jesus who loved him unconditionally? Far more questions than answers.

His emotional thirst was joined by a bodily thirst; a spiritual drink of the Living Water could have quenched them both. It is not for me to say that Simon was spiritually lost. He may have been. But I have known those whose addictions had weakened them to such a degree that although they loved God, they could not bring themselves to trust Him to save them from their enslavement.

For many years Simon had lived in a makeshift dwelling on the homestead of his parents. His father was, to all perceptions, a man of dignity and vision. He was widely respected as a community and church leader. The mystery of why Simon turned away from such a foundation remains unknown to me—perhaps to everyone. Not all who are offered the outstretched hand of a father's heart take it.

For every father-heart longing for restoration, for each one burdened by wayward children, I say, all answers are not found in you. You are the first but not the final influence your sons and daughters will experience. For those who spend quiet hours tormented by fear and failures, Simon's story says, "Father-hearts can be rejected, Judas did it too." To the Simons of this world, I say this: "Know that the Father waits to embrace and kiss you on your arrival home."

Simon stayed in our hometown his whole life, born and buried on the same square mile or so. It, amazingly, is possible to remain virtually unknown for such a long time in such a small place. Not that people didn't think they knew him—they did. They thought they knew all about him. But if you had asked many of them about Simon's thoughts, fears, hopes, hurts, they would not have known. Maybe no one asked.

Sometimes he would sit in front of the general store, a misfit store, relaxing in the sun. The bench outside along the storefront had been worn smooth by hundreds, maybe thousands, who had sat and talked on it. It harkened back to times of slower movement and longer reflection. It was a place to gather and everyone was welcome, even Simon.

The postwar release from stringency began a gold rush to prosperity. Now there was no time to lose in the building of bigger, better mousetraps to be sold to more and more people. Merchants and employees alike filled their lives with industry and its rewards, none of which were to be found on the bench. They drank different drinks than Simon, but their thirst was the same.

In the spring of 1960, my friend Randy and I packed our belongings in his 1956 Ford, and in the bright morning sun cruised west on Main Street and on out of town. As we passed the general store, old Simon waved at us. I think I waved back. It was the last time I saw him. I hope he finally satisfied his thirst. A man who tries that hard ought to.

Like I said, Simon was not trying to fit into society, but I was. I thirsted for acceptance, imbibing great amounts of pretense to achieve the feeling of belonging. A cousin of mine once called me "a con man extraordinaire." At the time he was right. I had concluded by the spring of 1960 that my best chances of being a somebody in this world lay beyond the boundaries of my hometown. The west coast of Canada became our destination.

I was unusually silent in the front seat as the miles slid by. The closest I can come to putting words to my feelings would be to say that I felt airborne. A weightlessness of spirit enveloped me as the gravity of religion, social-economic caste and personal conflicts were no longer able to keep me earthbound. I was flying into the borderless sky of my future on the wings of adventure.

The weightlessness was an illusion. Those weights would be replaced by others in time, every bit as heavy. Si-

mon had been seduced by alcohol; I was captured by the
need to belong and the need to be unfettered.

The contradiction is apparent. To belong is to become
committed. To be unfettered is to break all ties. I became a
man at odds with himself. I would knock on a door until
someone answered, then run like the wind so that I didn't
have to go inside and have the door close behind me. Relationships ran through my fingers like fine sand. I would
appear at opportune moments only to evaporate when relationships demanded more than they gave. My addiction
to being accepted and included was easily as strong as Simon's addiction to alcohol. The effects were not as imme-
diately observable, but were just as devastating in the long
run.

The day I left my hometown I was on the run. It was not
wrong to leave, but it was wrong to leave that way. Trying
to leave the child I was behind, I looked for new people and
new places to begin again. To relive my life. Like an animal
caught in a trap, I amputated a part of myself for freedom.
The price was high. To become someone else, you must
deny who you are. But who you *were* has everything to do
with who you *are*. The two are inseparably joined. The best
you can hope for is to be two people. For many years I lived
in denial of the pain-filled child I had been and the young
man I had become.

Ultimately, I came to accept—even love—the rejected,
angry kid I had been. I exposed my pretense. I faced my
addiction to acceptance. I realized that my reactions to the
restrictions of my past had only increased my isolation.

Slowly, I became the person I had been born to be. Summoning courage, I defeated my cowardice. I depended on God's strength and grace to change, to live righteously.

Slowly, the change came. It became OK not to have all the answers. Not to be the strongest, the best, the funniest. To be weak, to ask for help. Not to be right. Not to impress others or always please them. The person I manufactured I had never really liked. The son I discovered I liked a lot.

To be truly free from all of my isolation, I had to forgive those who had, even unknowingly, participated in excluding me from the things I longed to participate in. Forgive those who placed me outside their lives. Let others into yours. Especially let Jesus in.

Simon and I both lived life on the outside. We were shadows on the wall of life. We were both addicted by our efforts to soothe our pains and satisfy our cravings. We were both misfits. The only significant difference I see is that my thirst took me to the One who calls Himself the Water of Life. He said, "Whosoever thirsts, let him drink of the water of life, freely. If you drink the water of my life, you will never thirst again."

Would it help if I said that meant you need never remain thirsty again?

If you're thirsty enough, come.

If you're thirsty enough, drink.

When you come and you drink, you will live satisfied; you'll belong. He's the Water of Life and His name is Jesus. He's waiting now, just for you.

9   Pictures of the Bride

To be single and living with a broken soul is one thing; to be married in such an unhealed state is quite another. To be the father of a family in such inner turmoil is the worst of all three.

My broken heart, as I have told you, was unable to surround my bride or my beautiful children with love. I don't mean perfection, I mean love. Many, maybe most, feel as I did that they could rise above their early pain to begin again, to start over and do for their families what had never been done for them thus far. Without God's strength, this is indeed impossible. But to live in His strength requires a relationship of truth with oneself and with God. I was un-

willing to go so far. The truth was too painful and the vul-
nerability too dangerous.

I was out there on my own, trying to build a whole new
set of relationships on a broken foundation. Our home was
sure to crash—and it did. Not so others would know, you
understand. I was good at damage control. But it was written in my wife's and children's eyes. You could have seen it
there for yourself if you dared to look.

Pearl, my wife, and I got married in June, 1965. She was
nineteen and I twenty-one. Our marriage nearly didn't
make it. Conflict between us and between myself and our
oldest son shook the family framework. For years I pretended all was well. Slowly my strategies to survive began
to threaten the survival of us all. What started out being all
about my bride became about me. My heart was so selfish,
so deceived, that all others became a blur as I passed them
in my reckless rush to save myself.

Looking back carefully over the landscape of my life, I
can see how such a beautiful garden of marriage became
weed-infested. Many early seeds spread like unwanted
thistles through the years to come.

As a ten-year-old "man of the house," the chores had
fallen to me. Years of rising before the others on winter
mornings to stoke the great boiler furnace with coal and
wood, working many late nights washing floors with my
mother to feed our family, maintaining the vegetable garden behind our house—all of these were good for learning
a work ethic and for self-discipline. But for me they became the alternatives to the social activities I needed. To

these large responsibilities were added the emotional needs of my mother, which I sought to fulfill, and the unrelieved stress of poverty.

The net result of all of it was a silent but solid commitment to put my childhood on hold. Many years later, when grown, I would do as I wished, and woe to the one who gave me more responsibility—whether that person was my bride or not. When our home needed fixing or finances needed planning, I would say, "That's just not me." And the weight of caring for the family fell on Pearl's shoulders, which sagged more and more as the years went by.

The more disillusioned she became, the less affection she expressed toward me. It was not as if she held back; she didn't. I was offering her nothing to respond to. I was not laying a foundation of love for her to build on.

It is necessary to be emotionally connected in order to be honestly affectionate. Like many men, I too tried to cover my neglect of her with overt affection. It is one of the most offensive things a man can do to his bride.

Slowly Pearl lost the man she had married. My winning charm could no longer pacify her irritation or disappointment. She saw it as the manipulation that it was; silver-tongued devilry. My strategies of discounting her concerns, not taking her seriously, and turning a deaf ear to her frustration were pushing us to the edge of separation.

When this happened, a low grade of anger was always with me. My tolerance was low and my anger erupted unpredictably. My moods set the agenda for what would be a good or bad day in our home. I smoldered inwardly at the responsibilities of family life.

Our friends did not notice anything amiss. I was still the life of the party, but an ogre of the ordinary. This was no way to love my bride or keep my vows of marriage which I had openly declared before man and God . . . a covenant to love and protect her.

Look at the "snapshots" of my bride and me . . . how we began and where we have come to. We are completing our album these days. I hope you may be encouraged to add some new pictures to yours.

I'll always remember where I was when I saw her for the first time. In fact, I remember the exact spot where I was standing. That look changed the rest of my life . . . and hers.

Most events in history which capture our memories so completely are tragic in nature. This one was the beginning of a journey of adventure and love as we began our lives together.

Lest you think these thoughts emerge from a mind splashing about in some romantic froth, be assured they are not—not even close. Thirty-three years have passed since we were joined at the heart. It will take the rest of this story to decide whether you can believe me.

There is one indispensable truth I hope to convey to you. It could change your life and a few others. I want to be crystal clear about it; we may never talk again. What I have to say pertains to the brides of earth and the bride of heaven. The romance of earthly bridegrooms with their brides was meant to reveal the eternal love of Jesus, heaven's Bridegroom, with His chosen bride, the Church. "I saw the Holy City, the new Jerusalem, coming down out of heaven from God, prepared as a bride beautifully dressed for her husband" (Revelation 21:2).

The best way to love your bride is with the love of heaven. It takes a lifetime to love her that way, but if you choose to do that, even when you lose your bride, you get to keep the love. Love never fails.

Did you read that? Love never fails. It is inexhaustible and indestructible because God is love. I'm not talking about loving someone so she will love you in turn and you can live happily ever after. No, love is the unfathomable character of God, which transforms anything and everyone it touches. It changes the ones who open themselves up to it until their lives become a living opposition to everything that defeats or destroys here on earth.

For many years I did not know these things as reality because I would neither believe in this love nor receive Him. To receive this love, you must relinquish your life as your possession. Your life, self-owned, is much too small to contain eternal love or the riches it bestows. Endless love, eternal love, is not sustained; it sustains. It is not performed; it is lived. My journey into this eternal love was made walking beside my earthly bride. She was not my guide, but she was my companion.

It all began with a picture of her in my mind which developed as I looked at her across the room that day. There

were days along our journey so bright we wished they
would never end. There were nights so dark that, had I not
felt the touch of her hand on mine, I would not have
known she was there. And, but for the Lover of our souls,
our eternal Bridegroom, this story would remain untold.
There came a time in our lives when we abandoned Him,
seeking after other lovers for our souls, but He waited until
our loneliness drew us back to Him. He is faithful to the
end.

CLICK!

I stopped in mid-sentence to stare at her across the class-
room. Anyone who knows me knows I rarely stop in
mid-sentence. Those around me turned to look with me in
the direction of my distraction. "She's gorgeous," I murmured, more to myself than to anyone else. "I'm going to
marry that girl," I added.

Thirty-three years later, I still don't understand the intensity of attraction to a complete stranger. She was beautiful, no doubt. A classical beauty. Soft serenity on a finely
featured face. Eyes which played the music of mischief,
tenderness or girlish delight equally well. Her movements
were graceful, and her bearing has always seemed royal to
me, as if she had been born far below her station. My bride
has a defined dignity about her, supported by a keen mind,
balanced by careful wisdom. There is that in her which
commands rather than demands the respect of men. Being
with her, one observes an uncompromising integrity which
is not easily dismissed. I have never known anyone who

more easily wears the wardrobe of velvet or steel, as occasion may call for it.

My glance that day became a gaze, and in those first moments I saw enough to choose her for my bride. I wouldn't call it love. There was far too much of myself in my choice for it to be love.

So there she was, across the room, surrounded by her friends. She had a lot of them. Throwing her head back, she laughed, a sound like crystal touched by a silver spoon.

She seemed to know I was watching her, and once she turned to look steadily back at me. No flirtation, no rejection. A studying glance, cautiously curious and suitably brief.

When my sister died that winter she sent her condolences. It was a beginning.

We increasingly found ourselves in the same places, and then we began to plan our times together. On a crisp winter evening in early March of '63, we took a pot of hot chili to a small park on the outskirts of town. We talked and ate.

It seemed to me we had been friends forever, as if we were just taking up where we had left off. Being with her was the freedom of open places and the safety of a settled heart. Taking her hand, small and slender, we walked some distance along the country road which passed the park. We fell silent. Stopping, we stood looking at each other in the hazy moonlight.

The cold crystallized the clear night air, turning snow-flakes on her hair to sequins. "What?" she asked as lovers do when they look intently at each other.

"I'm thinking about you."

"Thinking what?"

"How beautiful you are." Words spoken by other lovers for millenniums were new again for us there under the spangled sky.

"And I'm thinking about you," she countered.

"And what's that?"

"How strong and caring you are . . . and handsome."

Our emotions required little adornment, as if we already knew what the other was going to say. I was the first to say it. "I love you."

"I love you too."

We asked each other for no explanations, no details. We had agreed on hidden terms. We each believed they would be filled to our greatest pleasure. The music that we heard inside ourselves was not written by the same composer but we agreed to sing the song of our lives together anyway. It was our song, and we would sing it till we got it right. Falling silent again, we sealed our venture with a kiss, maybe two. We held each other without words, something that can save a marriage.

Especially a winter marriage.

CLICK!

I looked across the living room at her. She smiled at me from the mirror she was facing. Her bridesmaids adjusted her tiara and fussed with her already perfect hair. The mys-

teries of marriage include the timeless radiance on the face
of a bride who knows the realities of selfish humanity but
lives in her chosen dream on her wedding day.

Broken promises forgotten, heartaches ignored, sad realities suspended, she lives in the momentary experience of
what life ought to be for those who choose each other. It is
a mystical place sent from the heart of God. Dreams of unending love. Dreams of beauty, dreams of chosenness,
dreams of vowed agreement of feasting, gifts and the intimacy of love. Dreaming for the symbols to become the
substance of her life. All of it crowned by the radiance of
the dream shining in the eyes of new beginnings.

In every place, in every culture, it is the same. The mystery of marriage is revealed by Jesus, the Lover of our souls.
His bride are those who receive His love, men and women
alike. Each bride on earth senses the eternal magnitude of
what she's doing. She senses what was meant to be hers
forever and believes, if only for a moment, that it is hers in
the here and now. Unconditional and endless love. I'm sure
my bride did. We vowed that we would love each other
that way. "In sickness and in health . . . till death do us
part." Jesus made that vow to His bride and kept it.

We preserved our memories with pictures taken in the
horticultural gardens near the church. It was apple blos-
som time. Promises of things to come. Blossoms which
should turn to fruit. Fruit tastes sweet; it satisfies your
hunger. It grows faithfully each year. That's what the bride
sees.

I still look at those pictures. Young, smiling believers arranged before the camera to remember the dream. It came down to two people in the garden. The final pictures taken were of us only. Then only the bride. I recall the photographer asking her to look at me standing beside him while he took her picture. She did. There was light in her eyes; she was surrounded by blossoms, surrounded by promises. We left the garden and went to be alone together.

CLICK !!

Winter came. Cold set in. Soft earth froze. Things became the way they were never meant to be. Strong winds rose and blew the blossoms to the ground. The pictures of those perfect people, now arranged upon our shelves, were rarely taken down.

I looked across the kitchen at her. She looked away. Dark-circled eyes. There was a question in her eyes she never put to words. *Am I still the one that you would choose? The only one on earth? Am I still in the pictures? Would you choose me again?* My words said "yes," my ways said "no."

Twenty years along our journey I wrote a song for her birthday. It told the truth which my life seemed helpless to convey.

Loving You

Loving you was never easy
Loving you was never hard
Like a villain or an angel
They both had to play a part

Like a butterfly in springtime
Like a river to a sea
Like a child before her years come
You need bondage to be free.
And so let me tell you of
The love that I hold
It's better by far
Than a treasure of gold
Your rights are unneeded
And mine are the same
When love is your servant
You don't need a claim.
Through the years I got to know you
Lines from some old-fashioned book
Tears and laughter, pain and pleasure
Like some pictures that we took
All the years we've spent together
All the dreams that came our way
Some came true and some just drifted
To the place we are today.

I wanted so much to tell her how sorry I was that her dreams were shattered. That *I* had shattered them. It hurt not to be her dream anymore. I wanted her to forgive me, but I chose my pride instead of her. How I ached to tell her that I was still the man who kissed her on a frosty night under the stars. We were both kissing our dream that night, and nowhere in the dream could be found the acts of our selfishness.

There came a day when the scales of love tilted, out-
weighed by the selfishness which had accumulated.
Bonding turned into betrayal, and we wandered in the
company of strangers. All we had left was our names and
our memories and our pictures of the bride.

CLICK !!

"You look great!" Pearl was radiant in the soft glow of
candlelight at our table for two.

"So do you."

Her eyes matched her smile. I couldn't take my eyes off
her. It felt like a night long ago in a park beside a country
road. The intimate dinner I had carefully planned and
cooked was arranged formally in the warm atmosphere of
our living room.

"This is so beautiful and so special," she said quietly.

Nodding assent, I smiled back at her. "Here's to us." I
raised my glass and took her hand. "To my lover and
friend, the most beautiful woman a man could ever know."
A tear slid down her face.

"I'm just happy," she explained needlessly. We clinked
our glasses. There was no "occasion" this evening, just the
company of two people joined at the heart.

I looked outside. Under the street lamp, the frost defined the birch tree in our front yard. The calligraphy of
winter, delicate and cold. Marriage of barren beauty. Frost
on a barren bough. How things had changed for us. Surrender to the lover of our souls had melted our hearts together. Our winter marriage had moved into spring: new
blossoms, new pictures of the bride.

She was the first to say it tonight: "I love you."

"I love you too," I answered. A tear slid down my face. We sealed it with a kiss. We had dreamed the same dream at last. "I will never let you go," I whispered.

"Nor I," she replied.

And waiting at the marriage supper table of the Lamb, the Father poured the wine of sweet release while the angels, looking through the windows, wondered at the beauty of the bride.

CLICK !!

Have you found the love that will never let you go, so that you will never let it go? You can be His bride today. You can be in His picture. The surrender of your heart to Him will fill you with a love unequaled on earth.

> O Love that wilt not let me go,
> I rest my weary soul in Thee;
> I give Thee back the life I owe,
> That in Thine ocean depths its flow
> May richer, fuller be.
>
> O Light that followest all my way
> I yield my flickering torch to Thee;
> My heart restores its borrowed ray,
> That in Thy sunshine's blaze its day
> May brighter, fairer be.

O Joy that seekest me through pain,
I cannot close my heart to Thee;
I trace the rainbow through the rain,
And feel the promise is not vain
That morn shall tearless be.

O Cross that liftest up my head,
I dare not ask to fly from Thee;
I lay in dust life's glory dead,
And from the ground
There blossoms red
Life that shall endless be.

—hymn by George Matheson and Albert L. Peace

10 The Wind and the Whirlwind

"**Y**ou are so hard-hearted!" my wife observed one February evening in 1984. I had just had a major confrontation with our oldest son. It had been ugly. My outburst had been out of proportion to the slight offense he had committed.

"Why are you on my case? He is the problem, not me!" I thundered at her. "He's got no respect for me or anyone else!" I continued.

"And you do? Where's your respect for him?" she implored.

It was an all-too-frequent scene in our home. Something was gravely amiss between my son and me. This story is about our rocky journey and the healing which became ours. I want to take you with us on our journey, which led through the wilderness and on to the promised land.

One thing is certain. When your marriage gets healed, so does your family.

I stood before my twelve-year-old son, who viewed me with confused defiance through red eyes, swollen with crying. "You and I will never get along!" he shouted.

It seemed at that moment that an evil, unseen power drove a dagger deep into my soul. I felt the lifeblood of what I wanted more than anything drain away. It was lost to me—forever, I thought.

This story, true, terrible, but ultimately hopeful, is the seed I wish to plant in all who have despaired of having or knowing the love of a father-heart.

The story of conflict with my son has its roots in the soil of the unresolved pain of my past. Let me say that although each one of us is profoundly influenced by his past experiences, especially those of his childhood, there comes a day when he is entirely responsible for his own choices; he is not merely a victim.

The early death of a beloved father, the difficult relationship with my mother, the introduction of poverty into my life, the religious restrictions I encountered and, above all, my own sinful response to all of these, shaped me into the man who abused his sons, daughter and wife. The ultimate choices and responsibility were mine and mine alone.

The first time I ever felt big as a boy was on my father's broad shoulders. From there I could look over the heads of men twice my size. It was a vantage point from which things usually hidden to me could be seen. On the occasion of which I speak, my father and I were standing outside the elephant enclosure of a visiting circus. The trainer was putting the great beasts through their paces. Pressing in, the crowd overshadowed me. All was lost from view as I felt trapped and excluded, clinging to my father's leg.

Suddenly he bent down, swept me upwards and placed me on his broad shoulders. Now I was higher than he! What I had longed to see was now unobstructed before my delighted eyes. There was no way to reach those heights apart from his simple, unselfish decision to lift me up higher than himself.

Most who read these words know the experience first-hand of riding upon a father's shoulders. Few indeed have been elevated to their father's hearts.

Those who have been in that joyful place have a clearer view of where they are in life and where they need to go. They expect to be lifted up when they feel trapped and iso-lated. Their faces reflexively look up, waiting for strong arms to reach for them. These who know the father-heart possess a solid and silent persuasion that they have been given what they need inside to deal with life, to give to oth-ers and to receive from them as they journey on. They are glad for who they are and extend that birthright to others also.

Those blessed to know a father-heart have heard an unforgettable message of unconditional love: "I will never leave you nor forsake you. Nothing can ever separate you from my love."

"I don't like one bit what you are doing, but you are irresistible to me"—this is the substance of bonding. The child's life is incomplete without the father and the father's without his child's.

Every father is equally equipped to love this way. Each loves inside his own personality. Some quietly, some exuberantly, a few creatively, most practically. The father-heart welcomes his child into some of his thoughts and seeks to know about his child's. He participates in the joys, sorrows, gains and losses and reveals his own in sensitive ways. A father-heart observes the life of his child and reflects upon it; he asks about and wants to know it.

He is not content merely to provide, protect and presume that all is well. He pursues relationship in many different ways. (Praying regularly for his child with real understanding is a primary part of fathering.) He neither panders to nor indulges his children. He prefers them to himself and presents them to the heavenly Father in his prayers. Looking for ways to bring out the best of who his child can be, he relates to his child in gentle honesty, firm conviction and open humility.

You may ask, "Why were you not like your father?"

The journey I walked beside him was short, the time I walked alone was long. The detour I took was one of rage and rebellion against the loss of my father. To know or share the father-heart requires the surrender of the will to the father-heart of God. When that happened in my life, I was able to father as I ought to have all along.

The foundation stones of good fathering had been laid in me by my father and others like him. These remained intact even though I built unmortared and shaky walls on them. It is never too late to rebuild, even though you may not get to complete the house.

I know of many men who have been crushed rather than lifted under the hand of the man they called Father. My first son Burke was one of these.

On February 18, 1966, I sat in the waiting room of Grey Nun's Hospital in Regina, Saskatchewan, Canada, awaiting the arrival of our first child. In the maternity ward nearby, Pearl lay in intense labor.

Outside, snowflakes large and lazy drifted to the ground. It was one of those nights on the prairies when beauty beats out the cold. Putting down my Greek text, I leaned back, closing my eyes to the bright fluorescence above me. The institutional clock on the wall traced the early morning hours. Alone in that room, I waited in the stillness; I was anything but still. I felt compressed between an unfinished youth and an early marriage, now fatherhood.

Understand that I was delighted with my new bride and even naively excited about parenthood. But my looming responsibilities and the replacement of myself as the primary recipient of Pearl's affections began to unsettle me deep inside. The tragic truth was that I was emotionally, mentally and spiritually completely unprepared for fatherhood.

"Be still and know that I am God." The words of Scripture came without invitation. I felt nothing of that peace. Instead, powerful emotions followed my thoughts. Exhilaration at the brink of birth, anxiety on the eve of fatherhood. Twenty-one going on fifteen; that was me. How I longed to phone my father to ask him what to do next.

A young doctor appeared suddenly at the waiting room door. "Congratulations, Mr. Toews, you have a beautiful son." He shook my hand. His "Mr. Toews" felt no different than when my uncles used to call me "Mister" to make me feel grown-up. "Everyone's fine," he continued. I knew what he meant. I wanted to tell this confident stranger that I was terrified, but I did what most men do. Squaring my shoulders, I braced my soul and walked briskly down the hall into fatherhood. No one meeting me would ever have guessed the anxiety I felt at facing the rest of my life as a father.

My son was beautiful! Pearl, in the first flush of motherhood, looked at him, then at me. They were both beautiful.

"He looks like you," she said. I couldn't tell, but it felt good to hear it. The anxiety retreated as I stepped into the falling snow later that night. A joyful energy rose up inside of me and I hollered at no one in particular. *I've got a son!* But I did not shout, "I am a father!" As I walked home I convinced myself that everything would be OK. I was a survivor who always managed to come out of tough situations smelling like a rose. This father-husband thing would be no different.

I trusted my instincts implicitly. My personal charm, quick-wittedness and powers of persuasion had never failed me yet. My spirit on the rise, I turned up the walk to our rented apartment, convinced all would be well. But my high-powered speedboat skimming across the pond of life was headed straight for the treacherous shoals of relational failure.

There was no friend I could call to tell about my son's arrival as my father had done, since I had not made any friends—not the kind built on a foundation of mutual caring and sharing. I chose "friends" who would amuse me, stroke my ego, be useful to me—but not hold me accountable in any way.

Neither was there any money to open an account for Myron Burke Toews, as my father had done for me. We had crashed our car in Pearl's eighth month of pregnancy. Our funds were exhausted to the point of poverty. Having enough food was our issue. We did give our son one legacy which I received from my father. We dedicated him in his second month to the Father in heaven to serve and love Him for his whole life.

Our life in that first year of marriage was a tense combination of celebrations and trials. We were both young and very much in love. I came from a chaotic background while Pearl had a fairly tranquil home life. She was slow to speak, wise, reflective and administrative, and I was verbose, impulsive and conceptual.

It would have been a tough mix to integrate in the context of a loving, stable community, let alone in our isolation and my immaturity. We plunged into a whirlwind of studying, working and now child-rearing amidst strangers. All of these under severe money shortages. It was a recipe for relational disaster. Only by a gentle silence did Pearl navigate the turbulent waters of my needy and selfish behavior.

I was not an ogre; I was a very broken man who had never honestly addressed the demons of his soul. They were attack dogs who were loosed on anyone who encroached on my carefully guarded pain. These "dogs" attacked by belittling efforts and opinions, stony silence, stinging sarcasm, public humiliation, private manipulation, loud, angry shouting, physical violence, withholding affection or "cutting criticism," attempting reconciliation by physical attention instead of genuinely asking for forgiveness. I would flush my guilt even with remorseful weeping, only to repeat the cycle soon after, instead of seeking help and committing to a change of behavior.

I loosed these attacks from my fortress of undisclosed and unaddressed pain. There are many today, as I was then, who resolutely refuse to acknowledge the pain which drives them to hurt others by their attitudes or behavior. They scoff at the helping, nurturing disciplines while running roughshod over those they care about.

Usually it takes years to inflict enough damage to break the cords of love, but the frazzled connection ultimately snaps. Often the offender stands shocked by the suddenness and totality of the breakage. A wife has an affair after years of criticism and neglect. A husband does the same after years of not measuring up to expectations, years of emotional manipulation. Sons and daughters reach adulthood and communication becomes an occasional obligation on the level of casual acquaintance. The dream of what might have been but never was calcifies into a relational stalactite in a dark, cold cave.

I was a pastor-in-waiting on a scholarship to Canadian Bible College. I had been recruited for the ministry. My ability to establish instant rapport with people was unusual. My track record in *staying* connected was abysmal. I learned to read people's reactions to me, to know how to charm and endear them to me, to be affirmed—to avoid at all costs the possibility of rejection.

We lost many potential friendships due to my aborting relationships when people offended or no longer amused me. My personal agenda included only endorsement of everything I did or thought. Anything else brought me in touch with my rejection. I outwardly gave but inwardly consumed.

If you had questioned my opinion or judgment, you would have been history. I expended effort and expense on total strangers while Pearl waited for me to attend to simple repairs around the house. Exercising compassionate patience with the delinquent children I cared for (if I liked them) was easy. My oldest son, by comparison, was allowed no margin of error.

Why was I living in the shadows? Why did I act like two completely different people? The detailed answer to this could fill a book, but the basic truth is this: I began marriage and fatherhood with a heart filled with unaddressed pain experienced from childhood to adulthood, and until it was addressed there was no hope of living like a whole person.

When he was born, my oldest son became my pride and joy, but also my responsibility. The inner vow I had made in my unfulfilled and restricted, overly responsible youth was this: "When I escape from all of this, I will recover my lost freedoms and do what I please, when I please."

Mature relationships, including marriage, do not allow for this viewpoint. Whoever has such thinking as his agenda is on a collision course with relational reality. The crash came shortly after my son was born. The initial pleasure of welcoming an extension of my life in the delightful person of Burke Toews abated when my wife was absorbed by the sponge of responsibility. Undefined resentment invaded me like a cancer.

As he got older I spent hours teaching him to excel at athletics, to play the games I was never allowed to play as a boy. I subconsciously hated the child I had been—powerless, socially excluded, unhappy. My son's behavior was modeled after my selfish immaturity. I saw a reflection of myself which I abhorred. The more he tried to please me, the higher I raised the expectations, until, as the Scriptures say, "hope deferred made his heart sick" (see Proverbs 13:12, KJV).

How could I unleash my angry disappointment in my life on a mere child? One of the frightening facts about our chosen evils is that they arise from a place in us which is hellish in its essence. We, one and all, are accessible to the killer, stealer and destroyer of life. Only the utterly efficient blood of Jesus can "cleanse us from all unrighteousness" and empower us by His indwelling spirit to overcome evil.

The child I cuddled, cradled and carried I also shook, yelled at and hit. It left behind a residue of insecurity and distrust.

Pearl tried her best to shelter the family from my unpredictable behavior and overcompensated for my inflexible approach to all things. Negotiation was weakness in my mind.

The years went by. Burke and my relationship became increasingly adversarial as he reached for independence. It became obvious to me that my son was alienated from me, and the distance between us grew larger.

In 1974 I was selected to help develop a new program for violent youth. To become a senior counselor on the Manitoba Community Treatment Team was indeed an honor. My acceptance letter, detailing my success in the area of working with dysfunctional youth, was delivered on a summer afternoon. That same evening, at supper, I ranted, raved and lost control in the discipline of my oldest son. He fled to his room and I stormed out of the house, letter in hand.

Crossing the road near our home, I walked the fairways of the Wildwood Golf Course. The irony was unmistakable. The contradiction between the man mentioned in my letter and the one who could not relate to his own son was painfully apparent. I was genuinely puzzled by the volume of rage inside of me which was directed at my son. Crying out to God, I begged him for freedom from my vortex of anger and guilt. I felt pinned by hidden forces.

"You see this letter?" I shouted at God late that night. "You see it and you see me. I can't go on like this, for his sake, Your sake or mine." My garbled words were lost in grief as I threw myself on the ground.

Such episodes became more frequent until I decided to seek wisdom from someone else. It was a small but crucial step. Most survivors trust themselves alone. They fear exposure of their weaknesses and faults; they conceal their ever-present pain under the most cavalier or controlled exteriors. Potential loss of acceptance drives them into a lifestyle of pretense except to those in their most intimate circle. It is onto those that they deposit their unbearable load of pain. Presenting these masks of self-assurance, their inevitable brokenness comes as a complete surprise to even their closest friends.

The man I sought out for help was a psychiatrist and a wise man.

I recall bringing my son Burke to him for rehabilitation. After spending an hour with Burke, the doctor sent him out to the waiting room and called me in. His words caught me by total surprise, such was the blindness of my pain. "Your son's only problem is you."

My reaction to his honest statement was predictable. He was blocking my number one agenda—total affirmation by everyone.

I listened but seethed inside, resolving not to return. I had no thought of my son's need, only my loss.

Fortunately, I came to my senses before the next appointment rolled around. I owe this kind and courageous doctor a debt of gratitude. He was faithful to his high calling. One of the questions he asked me shook me to my roots. Having related a bit of my background to him, I fell silent, waiting for his reaction.

"Why do you hate your brother so much?" he asked, looking at me steadily. Something inside of me welled up in anger.

"I don't," I replied much louder than I needed to for him to hear me.

"Your anger says otherwise," he replied calmly. He continued, "I believe when your father died, you became his 'father' and he became your responsibility. When your mother remarried, he came to live with you, becoming your responsibility again. I think you hate him for being what he is—footloose and irresponsible—and you would like to be that way. You can't show your anger toward him, because you believe that you must nurture and care for him as you were told to do as a mere child. So you have transferred the anger to your son!"

I was dumbfounded. This was no psychobabble. I knew it was the truth that, like a volcano lying dormant for years, still seethed inside. And now I knew. What I did now with the truth would testify to my character and integrity.

Because I was determined to be helped, my son and I are friends today. He has been able to know the love of a father's heart.

Alongside the psychiatrist's help, my pastor imparted some spiritual wisdom to me as well. When asked how to start practicing godly fatherhood, he replied, "Treat him the way God treated you."

God pursues those who sin against Him, to call them lovingly to repent, to reconcile with him. He forgives before we respond. He continues to bless our lives with goodness despite our rebellion. He remains faithful, righteous and loving whether we change or not. It was a recipe for recovery.

And so I began. The process was slow, and I dared not allow myself to depend on anyone else's responses. My nonnegotiable commitment was to do what was right regardless of my son's decisions or reactions. This formed the solid footing of success. I gradually became a changed man. I began to reap a harvest of peace as constructive behaviors were substituted for destructive ones. The only antidote to a curse is a blessing. I upheld most of the same values I had till then but I communicated them differently.

I began to ask more questions and offer fewer answers, make less dogmatic statements. Listen more carefully in order to understand. Apply discipline firmly and gently. I tried not to presume that people wanted to hear my opinion on everything.

Because my reactions were untrustworthy I would leave a developing confrontation, promising to return and resume when my emotions had settled down. This provided safety for all and allowed time to seek God for wisdom. It also provided room to consult with my wife, who had more wisdom and patience in the area of parenting.

The results were astounding as resistance began to dissolve and openness began to emerge. We still struggled, but now it was with issues rather than with each other. So after my son's fourteenth birthday, things began to change for us. However, the wind had become the whirlwind as the seeds of confrontative behavior I had planted in him were harvested by his sister.

Heidi endured from him the echoes of my sarcasm, intimidation and physical abuse. The heavy stone of my anger had landed in the middle of the family pond and the ripples were forming in ever widening circles. The elder brother who naturally would have protected, sheltered and promoted his sister began to dispense his pain into her perplexed soul. Years of disenchantment and quiet grief were not enough to contain her sadness. Cut off by the chasm I created from the one who could have been her strongest ally, she longed sadly and deeply for what should have become her rightful inheritance. The mercy of eternal God has and is restoring our hearts with Him and each other, but the losses are undeniable.

Donovan, our youngest son, suffered as his gentle soul lived in the relational whirlwind which surrounded him. Compliant, intelligent and sensitive, he took on negotiating peace. Subconsciously, he became the obedient son to reward us, as it were, for the rebellion of the elder. He suffered the effects of my sinful choices. His brother, who should have bonded with him as a male, became "like the grand canyon," awesome in his performance but distant and inaccessible. The waters of big brotherhood were muddied by the turbidity of his father's constant stirring.

Pearl paid a price unlike any of us. She was left alone to guard the gates of Burke's security. I thank God for her maternal faithfulness. Her reward awaits her. She opened her heart and hands to an abandoned son, giving him what hope she could that love would return in time. She was right. She stayed the course of wisdom, often risking my displeasure to plead the cause of her eldest son. It was love without earthly comparison. And although her strength was the God she trusted, her integrity held our family together with arms of love when my arms were wrapped around myself.

Last of all, I paid a price for my choices as a father with a small boy, a cost staggering in the magnitude of its loss. There are years of substance which have been emptied and sealed. I live today in the transparent joy of restoration, but, like Moses of old, can only gaze longingly into the promised land that might have been. I am forgiven, cleansed and transformed. My family will tell you as much.

But what I squandered is lost until all things shall be made new.

There are times when I peruse the pictures of our life together, carefully arranged in lovely albums. I stop in mid-album to put them back on the shelf, for the pain of those years is too much to observe. To many, we seemed like the perfect family, but I know the truth of those times.

The Scriptures say, "In quietness and in confidence shall be your strength" (Isaiah 30:15, KJV). This is not a comment on human personality. It refers to an attitude of listening and learning before God in order to become a recipient of His Father-heart and the ability to pass it on to those who await our fatherhood. My choices not to do so deprived my family of the enrichment they needed for themselves and each other. The natural bonding of loving in a safe environment, being able to be themselves, was not available to them.

Family life is an investment opportunity which narrows with each passing year. If you invest consistently and substantially and wisely, your entitlement at maturity is great indeed. The opposite is also true.

Today we are recovering hope. The rebuilding process has required the demolition of lies. I had to humble myself to look for and receive the help I found. Confession, repentance, forgiveness and loving honesty were the watchwords of this journey. The prize is in view and the rewards delightful. It's working.

I applaud the bravery of any who will decide to end the cycle of "fatherless" living, to begin to receive and release the father-heart. God stands ready to forgive your sins—past, present and future—to heal your broken heart and empower you to love from the fullness of a father-heart.

The harsh wind of cold rejection has become a warming, gentle wind of loving relationship. The whirlwind has subsided before the raised-up hand of the one whom winds and waves must obey when He says, "Peace, be still."

11   Orphan Hearts

et me tell you about the orphan hearts I tried to
father. They were abandoned, tattered souls, lost
along the road of life, unwanted and unnurtured. Some were
vicious, some demonized and some were simply abandoned
by everyone. Some had killed, all had conned. My heart ached
for them and still does.

One of the axioms of what could be called heart-health
wholeness of mind and emotion is, "You can only restore
others relationships to the extent yours has been healed." A
tragic fact I have observed over many years of social work
and counseling is that a great many people who enter these
occupations learn the skills of relational knowledge aca-
demically, but they themselves remain unchanged in character or behavior. This certainly was my situation. But life

has a way of exposing frauds, and time exposed me. I did not set out to perpetrate a fraud, but I was self-deceived. Even when I saw my brokenness in practice, I refused to face the truth about myself and get help to change. I say "get help" because no one I have ever met is capable of truly changing for the good without the help of others. So I was not what I appeared to be, a professional restorer of relationships. I needed help, and I got it when I faced the truth about myself.

Can you help others when you yourself are still broken inside? To a certain extent you can, in a superficial kind of way. Can the blind lead the blind? No. They will both end up in the ditch of life, watching others pass them on their way to the city of restored relationships. Why don't you get help today? It could change your life for the better forever.

I know many ministers, social workers, even counselors who refuse to get help. Their pride and self-deception fools no one but themselves. The people who come to them for help never find wholeness under their tutelage. They are like prostitutes of pain. Their help is momentary and deposits their clients back into their misery.

Because healing for me and my family came through the door of truth, others could find restoration through our experience.

One of the most energizing and encouraging truths ever presented to me is that God is the grand economist. He wastes nothing. All the pain, suffering and loss which we would throw away, He carefully reinvests into the lives of those who allow Him to do that. The years of conflict with my oldest son and the healing which followed makes me believable to others when I say, "God will restore you to health if you pay the price for change."

Men who are in despair over their marital failure, listen and believe that there is hope for them when I share my story. Over the past fifteen years I have seen many believe and change because God did not waste the brokenness in my life.

The orphans were a part of my life which framed this truth as an unforgettable priceless portrait of beauty. They were kids and young men who had fatherless lives. They were desperate and defeated. They were prime candidates for a father's love. I tried to give that to them. Here are the stories of a few.

Pushing open the chipped-paint door of the Carter Café, I stepped inside. Smoke, hanging visible like blue fog, burned my nostrils. It wasn't the only blue thing in the air. Vulgar cursing from a gathering of rowdies came from the last booth in the dingy room. They seemed to be celebrating something.

I glanced at the large woman perched on a bar stool behind an ancient cash register. Tilly blended well with her surroundings. A cigarette hung from her shapeless lips. Underarm sweat stains gave evidence of a body long since abandoned to neglect. Tilly never left the café. She lived in a room or two at the rear of it and had everything delivered. Her face, sagging and mottled, was a mask of melancholy. Having long since dispensed with the civilities of restaurant service, she shuffled about with a coffee pot permanently stained a deep brown, grunting at the patrons who chanced her cooking. Carter Café clientele were mostly locals who knew her. I was a stranger and she looked at me more closely. I looked at her. "Hi." I tried to sound upbeat. "Where should I sit?" I asked.

I had already embarrassed myself. No "wait to be seated" sign in this place. Tilly didn't move, didn't say a word. She pointed a pudgy finger to the booth opposite the rowdies. Every finger on her hand had a diamond ring on it. Her nails were long, shiny and sharp. Bright crimson, they reminded me of drops of blood as her hand hung down. The obvious extravagance of her diamond-laden hands seemed to contradict the rest of this place.

Six pairs of unfriendly eyes followed me as I walked toward the booth which Tilly had indicated. The rowdies fell silent. Conspicuous in my white middle-class manner, dated by my slacks and cardigan, I sat down and focused on my coffee.

"Something smells like pork in here," sneered the one I had heard the rest call Jacko. His hostility was practically tangible.

So that was it. They had looked me over and decided I was a cop. "He's a little late," one of them continued. "He should've been around last night."

"Shut your gob, you sawed-off runt." Jacko lashed out at a short, flat-faced kid with the undesirable name of

Pinky. Pinky stopped as if he had been crunched by a billy club.

A tall, dapperly dressed kid named Stick rose to leave. "Can't keep the girls waiting." Speaking slowly, he feigned sophistication.

He looked at me through hooded eyes, just a hint of a leer on his young face. Well groomed, nattily dressed, with a watch fob gracing his right hip, he seemed as out of place as I did. He was and he wasn't. The group and the slick stick were having a business meeting. He was their fence. They were thieves of fortune. Tilly was a lonely woman who shut her eyes and ears and wore their spoils of war on her hands.

Stopping to whisper something to Tilly, Stick flashed a V-sign, lit another cigarette and left the booth of idolaters behind.

"He's so smooth," exulted a skinny kid called Poker, who had been quiet until now.

"Something you'll never be," rejoined Pinky. "You are a motherless squid and gutless to boot."

Poker faced his oppressor. "Oh yeah, who ripped the old lady last night?"

Jacko looked hard at me, and with one motion he back-handed the unsuspecting Pinky flush across the face.

Tilly was on them like an irate mother bear. At an unlikely speed for a woman of her size, she reached the booth, rasping filth like a drunken sailor. "Settle down now or I'll toss the whole lot of you out on your brainless heads!"

Deftly, she flicked her wet dishrag, snapping it at Jacko's ears. "Especially you, scuzball, or next time I call the cops."

Tilly and Jacko were alike. They offered the others their acceptance at a price, living by a code which protected their turf, their way.

I surveyed the unlikely gathering before me. They needed and rejected one another at the same time, like hyenas who hunt together then fight over the meat. I wanted them to know what I knew. As a new father, something inside of me wanted to love them in fatherly ways. To tell them, to show them they could live free of fear, free from sin's power, free from darkness, forgiven and loved unendingly by the Father of light. They watched me as I walked to the front door. "I'm paying for all their stuff," I told Tilly.

"I wouldn't know why," she growled. "You got too much money?" Her eyes asked me the question she wouldn't put into words: *What's in it for you, mister?* She wouldn't have believed me if I had told her.

The kids—Jacko, Pinky, Poker and the others at the Carter Café—were essentially fatherless boys. They all had fathers but not so you'd notice. More accurately, they were emotional orphans. They were disconnected from their fathers, unbonded, unloved and misguided with all the predictable results of such abandonment.

In 1966, I began to reach out to children who were experiencing fatherlessness. After more than thirty years of doing that, it is my strong conviction that the vast majority of youth problems could be eradicated by consistent and loving fathering. The thirst for a father-child relationship has become intense in our world.

The delirium over the lack of that relational water has birthed a generation, a great many (some surveys say close to fifty percent) of which live by the side of life's roads. They have no direction, so they drift. No security, so they seek escape. No motivation, so they become slackers. No dreams, so they live for today. No love, so they hate randomly. No guidance, so they rebel. No self-respect, so they despise. No hope, so they commit suicide. No absolute truth, so they live with lies. What will their children be like? Generation X, if we use that label, was around in 1967, albeit in smaller numbers.

A thirty-year parade of the fatherless passes before my eyes today. Astoundingly, at least half were well supplied with food, shelter, clothing and the toys of life. These were the angriest of all. Perhaps because they knew material prosperity was an artful dodger, making promises it could not keep. In many cases, the love of money had replaced the love of children, who were left hungry for love and disillusioned by life. With very few exceptions, as these children grew older, they filled their relational emptiness with peers equally distraught at their abandonment.

The orphans knew nothing of a father's heart. Some did not know who their fathers were. Many had fathers who abused them. This, of course, was worse than having no father at all. One evening I was teaching on the love of the heavenly Father for them. Bulldog, a boy known for his vicious streak, pulled up his T-shirt, revealing large purple welts on his back. "This is how my father loves me," he laughed. No one else laughed, and his eyes were alive with hate as he spoke. The one who should have cared for Bull-dog had cursed him with his hands as well as his heart. Thoughts of a loving heavenly Father did not come easily to him.

Some of the orphans' fathers were in prison, and those believed that their future lay in prison too. The title "orphans" meant total abandonment not only by their fathers but by their mothers as well. Usually, their mothers tried to provide some sort of nurture. Far too often, however, their mothers were abused and abandoned along with their children. Most of these mothers I knew were angry and hopeless about their lot, so their nurture didn't feel like nurture.

Eventually, the kids all got around to asking me the question on each of their minds. Why do you care? Are you getting paid? Grudgingly, I had to admit that I was but I explained that I really did care about their lives. It took a long while for them to believe that. Through the years, many kids like the orphans have asked me to adopt them. They are ravenous for love; it was painful to tell them I could never be their dad.

I would see them trying hard to please me, even as rebellious as they were. Not daring to hope for love after all they had been through, they often pretended not to need it. The orphans wore self-contempt like a ragged suit. They rejected their own bodies and inflicted damage on themselves in a variety of ways. Revealing the depth of their personal pain, they slashed their wrists and arms, burned themselves with lit cigarettes, tattooed messages of hate, and at times drank themselves into oblivion.

The only weapon I have ever known capable of breaking the cycle of hate is genuine loving relationship. During the course of caring for abandoned children, I have watched some incredibly patient and heroic people love them into health and wholeness.

Love prevails over hate. Not all kids who were profoundly changed by love became Christian believers. I have seen some miraculous changes in the lives of those who believed in Jesus Christ. These were not only changed for time but for eternity. Even those who believed, however, were not able to sustain changes in their lives without wholesome relationships.

Just how is this new life imparted to you?

John explains it more fully. "He was in the world and though the world was made through him, the world did not recognize him. He came to that which was his own but his own did not receive him" (John 1:10-11).

John was arguing that the man historically known as Jesus was in fact Creator God. Christ's coming differed from ours in an important way: in being born on earth, Jesus came to territory He already owned. He was the rightful Lord of the earth, the Lord over everything and everyone in it. Rather than becoming a peasant, He could have come as divine judge and destroyed the earth, consumed it. Instead, Jesus chose to spend nine months in Mary's womb and to experience to the full extent our human condition—all to break the evil curse that lay upon us. As man, He bore the full horror of that curse, shattering the power of evil that plagued humanity because of His love for us. In so doing, Jesus opened the way to the new life and identity He now offers us. How do we receive that act of supreme love? How do the new life and identity become our own?

John continues to explain:

> He came to that which was his own, but his own did not receive him. Yet to all who received him, to those who believed in his name he gave the right to become children of God—children born not of natural descent, nor of human decision or a husband's will, but born of God. (John 1:11-13)

The new life and new identity hinge on faith. The blessings and benefits of a world to come are for all who receive Him and believe on His name He gives the right to become children of God. God adopts them, but He does more. In some mysterious manner He sires them; His own life enters into them.

How does it happen? What does it mean to receive Jesus? What do the words "believe in His name" mean?

We receive Jesus by doing the opposite of what the world did when it rejected Him. When He "was in the world," when He "came to that which was His own," Jesus encountered largely a lack of recognition and even outright rejection. Religious leaders viewed Him with hostility and murderous hate; the populace offered Him fickle admiration; the bewildered civil authorities afforded Him no protection, sacrificing Him to political expediency.

Jesus knew it would happen . . . and embraced what was to happen for the greater purpose which brought Him to live among us.

To receive Him we must do the opposite. We are to recognize who and what Jesus truly is—our owner and the Lord of our planet. We must bow the knee before Him as our rightful Lord and Master. In this way we reverse what happened historically. If Jesus is who and what He said, we can afford neither indifference nor hostility.

But we need to do more. We "believe in His name." His name "Jesus" means receiver, deliverer, champion, Savior.

In dying, Jesus championed our cause and paved the way for our salvation. To "believe in His name" is to believe in what His name means and to trust Him. It is to place our confidence in Him and trust our destiny to Him. It is to recognize that Jesus can do for us what His name implies and to count on Him to do so.

Jesus once said, "Whoever comes to me I will never drive away" (John 6:37). He wants us to understand that He will always and gladly receive whoever comes to Him for help. If this is so, how much greater is the hope of those who come to submit to His authority and count on His power to impart new life!

To be born again is to be "born not of natural descent, nor of human decision or a husband's will, but born of God." This birth is no physiological process but a supernatural one—the infusing of supernatural life into our bodies, the life of God Himself.

This infusion means that God Himself became incarnate within us, for what He is offering is more than life, more even than divine life. It is divine life in the form of His very person. God offers Himself—not just a part or a portion of Himself but His whole self. This is a great mystery, I grant you, but one taught by the Bible and the Christian Church down the ages.

The orphans heard the truth but paid little heed. They seemed unmoved by Bible teaching. They had learned not to trust words nor the people who spoke them. It remained necessary for the message and the messenger to become the same. It is the goodness of God that leads us to repentance (Romans 2:4). That is how "orphans" become fathered again. They need someone to love them.

The price to be paid for such restoration is high to the one who reaches out. In the call of Christ it can be no other way. The only way to find life is to lose it. The life you lose is yours, the life you find is His. Religion has found substitutes for loving. Some of them are generous giving, moral living, gifted expressions, even preaching and praying.

Those are all good things, but they are not substitutes for loving people. Everyone who claims to follow Jesus is required to reach out to broken people. Those who do not believe this fool themselves, for Jesus said, "As the Father has sent me, I am sending you" (John 20:21).

Not everyone should work with gangs. But every disciple of Jesus must reach out to the poor and needy at personal inconvenience and cost. It must be clearly said that humanitarian sacrifice and service can bring about changes in people, even in whole societies. However, only the indwelling presence of God can revolutionize a person's heart for this lifetime and the next.

Today we live in a world populated by those waiting for the Father-heart of God to be revealed. How and where will they see it? The fields are white already for harvest (John 4:35, KJV). Pray the Lord of the harvest to send workers, including you, to reap for Him. The Father-heart of God offers loving care, given in Jesus' name, to the fatherless. True, undefiled religion is to care for the fatherless and widows in their affliction (James 1:27). We are called to demonstrate His love in practical ways to those around us, sharing the truth of the gospel at every opportunity. Living with less that others may have more.

The orphans watched and waited and wondered as we nurtured them on love and the words of God. Some believed and kept believing. Others agreed and went unchanged. All of them got a glimpse of the Father-heart.

Jacko did not give up his place as king of the mountain easily. He had a lot of trouble relating to God as his father. Even on a hot summer day he did not remove his shirt. I asked him about it after we knew each other well. What he showed me I can still see. It made me sick.

His father, in a drunken rage, had tied his hands over a beam in the basement of their house and left him there for hours. He had beaten him with electric cords and the marks had never gone away. The worst scars were on his heart. They never healed. Jacko caught pigeons under a city bridge. I discovered him nailing the poor creatures to a garage wall for target practice. Years later he murdered a girl while strung out on mescaline. He remains in prison still.

Pinky and his family were immigrants. They spoke, ate and in general lived differently than others. He grew up fighting his way in and out of school yards. His mother insisted on putting garlic in his lunch. It alone ostracized him from his classmates. Desperate for acceptance, he threw away his lunches and began to steal food. Thus began a juvenile life of crime. An intelligent boy but emotionally distraught, he was placed in a class of slow learners. There he was received as an equal at the price of antisocial behavior.

I loved Pinky. He had the soul of a lamb and would follow anyone who would include him. Many times he would ask me to tell him what my life in the country had been like. A wistful look would come into his large, doelike eyes.

"It must have been like heaven," he would say. "Did you have a lot of friends?"

I wanted to say no but admitted to some.

"I've never had a friend," he replied.

"Isn't Poker your friend?" I asked.

"I don't think so," the answer came. "He's Jacko's friend."

Pinky received Jesus but was too weak to stay out of jail. Every time I visited him he would ask me to sing the song I had taught him. He said a warmth came over him when I did, and he would close his eyes and smile as I sang. When

I finished he would slowly open his eyes. "I feel good—warm—inside when you sing," he would say.

He had been touched by the Father-heart of God. He finally belonged to someone.

Joeboy's family were Satan worshipers. He recalled them dedicating him to the occult priesthood at seven. He would sometimes go into a catatonic state, from which he would emerge in sudden, blinding rages. He was slightly built but could intimidate much larger boys than he, who wisely believed he would stop at nothing to get revenge for affliction brought upon him by others. Joeboy had been sexually abused beyond description. Thus traumatized, he escaped into other personalities, and in his teens began to inject himself with anything that would numb the pain and make him feel good.

The side of Joeboy few saw was that of a baby. He was maternally gentle with animals, speaking tenderly, rocking them. Stroking the furry face of a kitten, he crooned lullabies. More than once I found him sucking on a baby bottle, curled up in his bed. Joeboy's uncontainable rage was a wall over which he could never see the Father-heart of God. He hung himself while in prison at the tender age of nineteen.

Wesley, alias Weasel, came to the city from a remote northern town where his father and mother were missionaries. They served all but their own family. The physical discipline laid upon the body of Weasel was of such extreme that he lost continence. He was made to eat his own waste by the man he called father—by the man who called others to the heavenly Father.

Wesley (I never could use his nickname) was highly intelligent, but so emotionally damaged it was not noticeable except in written tests. His only physical intimacy had been violent and so he bothered the other boys until they beat him.

When the Jesus People came to the streets of Winnipeg, they began to love Wesley. After being taught in things of God, he believed and received Jesus. One night he boldly proclaimed his faith. The boys who mocked Wesley in his new faith slipped several hits of LSD into his soft drink. They waited for him to "lose" his mind. It should have left him insane or at least hospitalized. It didn't faze him. As the Lord of life said, "When they drink deadly poison, it will not hurt them at all" (Mark 16:18). There were many who believed that night because of God's protection of Wesley.

The Father-heart of God found Wesley, despite his history of abuse. Nothing could separate him from the love of the Father's heart in Jesus Christ, not even his own father. Wesley never walked in wholeness but he loved the Father.

Stoney was named after the unchanging expression on his face. It applied to his heart as well. I spent several years caring for Stoney. I don't think he spoke more than six words to me in as many months. He would grunt in two different ways which I learned were yes and no. Even when he drank straight, hard liquor, he said not a word but went on sprees of property destruction and fighting. He would

disappear for days without explanation and reappear as if
he had gone to the corner store. He had been assigned to
my care as a senior counselor in a program for the rehabilitation of violent youth.

Stoney eventually trusted me enough to discuss the
nightmare which had been his youth. I wondered at times
why he had not escaped it all by suicide, which many like
him had. Stoney had lived on a reserve. At six, his grandfather sent him with two large pails to haul water from the
village pump a mile distant. The trip took him the better
part of a morning. Upon arrival home with whatever water
had not been spilt, Stoney's grandfather would inspect the
pails. If any debris was visible he would tip the pails and
the little boy would finish off his day by hauling two more
buckets. And so it went for sixteen tortuous years, until liquor and rage took him to the "safety" of an adult jail.

Stoney did not know that sex had anything to do with
love although I could tell he was a boy of sensitive nature
under all that anger.

One night, his girlfriend attempted suicide by jumping
in front of a car. Stoney, by this time eighteen years old,
snapped. High on a combination of angel dust and booze,
he returned to the halfway house where he lived in a state
of ugly grief. With an iron bar, he destroyed everything he
could. Wherever he saw the reflection of his face in mirrors
or windows, he smashed them with his fist, so intense was
the hatred he felt for himself. The house flooded as water
pipes were broken. Every window lay in fragments on the

floor, and the winter wind turned the place as cold as a tomb.

The other residents fled and the police came. It was just after midnight when my phone rang at home. The sergeant explained, "We want you to come down to see if you can get near to the kid. He's holed up on the second floor. We don't know if he has a gun up there and we don't want to hurt him."

The ride downtown was spent praying for wisdom and peace to prevail. "No one loves Stoney as much as You do, Father. Don't let this be the end for him," I prayed.

Five cruiser cars with flashing lights surrounded the house. Twice as many police were gathered on the main floor. At the rear of the house I climbed the fire escape. The door was open. Apprehensively, I entered, calling Stoney's name. It was dark except for some light filtering in from the street lights outside. Then with a start I saw him not ten feet in front of me. The iron bar, like a scepter of violent hate, was held by this young prince of pain. His eyes, wild with demonic despair, blazed out of a face covered in blood.

"It's over for me," he groaned. "What do you want?"

"Stoney, listen to me." And then I said something I deeply doubted would carry any power at all let alone penetrate the drugs or despair. "Stoney, I love you." I had said that to many people in my life. Sometimes sincerely, a few times passionately, sometimes hypocritically, even casually. This time I said it desperately. What I saw before me was a sweet baby who had become a child of torment, poised on the brink of hell. Too many hatchets were left to bury. His one ray of hope for some kind of love was slipping from his grasping heart.

My words seemed like a feather when I needed a hammer. I said it again, "I love you and I won't leave you tonight."

It was an echo of what my Father in heaven had said to me. Somewhere in that bloody darkness the feather touched an uncalloused place in his soul. The iron bar clattered to the floor. Stoney staggered forward and threw his arms around my neck. The blood from his many cuts mingled with the perspiration on my face as I hugged him. He sobbed great, heaving sobs as years of tears were released from deep inside of him.

Eventually his cries subsided as he remained in my arms. Then he looked at me in the darkness. "Will I have to go to jail?"

"Yes, Stoney, you will."

"Will you stay with me tonight?"

"Yes, Stoney, I will."

Again the words came to me, "I will never leave you nor forsake you. Nothing shall be able to separate you from my love which is in Christ Jesus our Lord." There we stood. Two men separated by every social criteria one could name, united by one single thing—love. It was, is and always has been the truth. The love of the Father's heart can cross any barrier, break down any wall and conquer the worst hell can wreak. The Father's heart is in search of orphan hearts. They are irresistible to Him and His love is irresistible to them.

Stoney's heart melted in the warmth of love as time went by. Today he is a husband and father. His children are not fatherless; they are not orphans.

"I will be a father to you," says the Lord, "and you shall be my children" (see 2 Corinthians 6:18).

12 Angel in Dirty Jeans

I left home while it was still dark and began the three-and-a-half hour ride to Winnipeg. It was an "in and out" trip, seven hours of highway driving with several hours of city driving between, supplies to pick up, people to see, business to conduct. Somewhere in the middle of it all, I needed to accomplish my main reason for the trip: My doctor had insisted I get a bone scan to establish the reason for a persistent pain in my lower back which had left me unable to do even light labor.

Hospitals hold an abundance of unhappy memories for me, not the least of which are my father's and sister's deaths, my mother-in-law's recent passing and some stays of my own. Fortunately, as with most other difficult experiences of life, they are counterbalanced by events which adjust the scales of human experience. The births of all three of our children were hospital experiences, which produced joy in immeasurable quantities. Just the same, I would prefer to stay clear of hospitals.

I walked through the doors of the hospital and was directed by a pleasant receptionist to the nuclear medicine ward, GG3. It sounded like a department of the Pentagon rather than something relating to my well-being. The corridors were alive with people.

I entered a low ceilinged, dingy hallway with a row of vinyl-covered chairs arranged along one wall. The drone of the PA system pages gave me a feeling of non-identity. How big was this place, anyway? Electronic voices and nuclear medicine are hard to reconcile with an atmosphere of healing—certainly the personal sense of it.

All the vinyl chairs but one were taken by people who seemed as reluctant to be there as I was. I hoped my 9:30 appointment wouldn't turn into an 11:30 appointment, since my experience told me that doctors have been given the historical right to keep you waiting. (It could even be a piece of legislation somewhere.)

My latest fear evaporated when my name was called. For the multi-thousandth time in my life, they pronounced my name wrong and I responded as I always had, by answering to it.

The male nurse briefed me as to procedure. His manner was civil and hinted at attempted warmth. He could not be blamed, I thought. His visitors were in various conditions and stages of illness and his job function is repetitive and mechanical. It must be hard to keep a compassionate bearing about you. Jeff, which was his name, was efficient as he injected the needle which would highlight my bones with radioactive dye and make it possible to get clear skeletal images of my body.

I thought of the searching eyes of God to whom nothing is hidden, who sees and knows my spiritual condition as no one does, whose gaze penetrates my efforts to conceal my careful coverings, my silence, deceit and pretense. I thought about standing speechless before His full revelation one day, not more than a handful of years away. It also occurred to me how important it was for me to walk in the light of His truth here, now, while I had choices to make. I didn't want to be ashamed at His coming. Would I have to shift my gaze from His, or could I look joyfully, fully into His face and thank Him for the grace to live honestly, in love, without hypocrisy?

The injection done, I left, to return later in the afternoon for the x-ray session. My schedule was cramped and time was at a premium.

A higher-than-average number of miscues and irritations, delays and forgettings increased the pressure on my already weary body. Picking up my mail, I opened an envelope containing a check, kept the envelope and discarded the check in the trash bin. This led to frequent trips between the car and post office, searching everywhere for the lost paper. Finally, logic overcame panic and a scrutiny of the garbage revealed it lying crumpled within arm's reach.

Walking to the car, I chastised myself for having wasted so much of my precious time.

It was dark again as I left for home two hours later than I had planned, dreading the three-and-a-half hour ride ahead of me. Curving roads seem endless in the dark. Concentration was crucial, though my body craved sleep.

Then my headlights picked up the outline of a hitchhiker on the gravel shoulder. *Who would be crazy enough to hitchhike in winter at night?* I wondered. The word "crazy" was mine, the term "desperate" never occurred to me. It is not my habit to give rides to hitchhikers, especially at night. But something inside of me practically applied the brakes for me as I pulled to the side and waited for the figure running towards the car.

He eased into the front seat, panting with exertion and thanking me for stopping while I was still wondering why I had. My eyes appraised him—his name was Keith—briefly in the light before the door closed. He was boyish-looking. I guessed him to be around twenty. His freckled face had an easy smile but dark circles surrounded his eyes. He removed his toque to reveal short, dark hair and an earring in his left ear. I was surprised at his thin jacket, given the cold wind he had been facing. The jeans he wore were ragged and dirty. A knapsack completed his attire. He hadn't had a bath for a while by the smell of it. I wondered if my "do-gooder" instinct had me busy rescuing another hard luck case or whether it was God who had drawn me to this young man for the purpose of showing him compassion.

We began to talk, seeking and offering general information—safe stuff. We didn't linger long on the trivia of life before Keith began to disclose the way things were with him. Those with grief and trials seem to want to share them with me. I have come to accept this experience as God's will in my life, for the purpose of channeling His love, mercy, encouragement and compassion through my life to others. It's sometimes a blessing, sometimes a duty, often inconvenient and occasionally costly. But whenever I listen to His command to do so, a deep-settled joy becomes mine. An awareness of the pleasure of a father with his son sensitizes my spirit, and I know a foundation of satisfaction which cannot be moved.

The miles slipped by, and Keith told me why he was crazy and desperate enough to be hitchhiking in winter, at night. *Night and winter describe his accumulated years rather well,* I thought to myself as he talked. The tragedy of violence and alcohol, ending in divorce, was his legacy. A father who roughnecked in the oil fields, a mother who tried her best, though abandoned herself, to raise an angry son.

Seeking recognition unavailable through his father, Keith lunged into a blur of weeks, months and years of drinking, fighting and resisting his mother. He began the cycle earlier than most, at the tender age of twelve. By the time he turned fourteen, his mother sent him to his father to preserve her sanity, unable to control him, having lost control herself.

The episode left him bitter and full of hate for a mother who, in my limited perception, did the only thing a mother could have done, which was to send him to his father.

I interrupted him to ask if he had ever forgiven her. He was taken aback by the question, too consumed with his commitment to blaming her to even consider the option, let alone the importance of such an act. I didn't venture to ask if he had ever asked her forgiveness, although I wanted to.

Life with his father was a treadmill of trying and failing to please, seeking desperately for approval by imitating the tough exterior of the man who should have loved him into strength and manhood but didn't. Now, due to a recent crisis, Keith was returning to Ontario to see Debbie. Debbie was a twenty-seven-year-old woman who had borne their child, named Doug. I shuddered as I thought of the emotional inheritance of this child and prayed he would be helped by God early in his unpromising life.

"I love Doug," Keith explained as his voice quavered. "He does such cute things," he added.

This young man was light-years away from readiness for fatherhood. I tried to be enthusiastic about his delight but sadness was seeping into my heart. After twenty-five years of trying to help young men and women like Keith, I realized the odds of his son having a whole, healthy life were slim indeed.

"Debbie's got cancer of the bones," he suddenly blurted out. His voice trembled and his words came out tightly through his choked-up throat. "Her pastor phoned me.

She's gotten religious and I think she attends a 'fun gospel church' or something like that." I was thankful for the comic relief. Keith continued, "I promised I'd be there to take her into the hospital on Monday morning."

It was my turn to swallow hard. Here he was, twenty-two years of confusion—abandoned, hurt and rejected—and he was still trying, in some way, to be the man he was born to be. I marveled at the Light that lights every man that comes into the world. He was a broken heart on a mission, sharing his broken heart, in his own way, with someone else. *There must be a sermon in there somewhere*, I thought to myself.

"I can't talk about this much," Keith said. "It depresses me every time I do."

Silently I reflected on God's purpose for me in this unusual encounter. Was God telling me through this troubled young traveler to look beyond my difficulties and trust my Heavenly Father to meet my need?

My father-heart ached for this young warrior who had lost so many battles but was still in the war. I invited him for supper, a shower and a warm bed. He accepted with much gratitude. I reflected momentarily on the last time such gratitude had found its way into my heart for such simple pleasures. How often I had murmured complaint about my days as I sauntered to bed with too much dessert and not a word of thanksgiving to my "heavenly landlord."

My wife welcomed the young stranger with motherly care, and more than once I saw him glance longingly her way. Was he thinking what life could be like with his mother if he would only forgive? Wanting to respond somehow to the kindness he was being shown, Keith pulled two well-worn CDs from his bag and handed them to me. They were romantic country songs.

He groped for appropriate expressions to accompany his gift. "I like these CDs. They have love songs on them mostly. Debbie and I used to enjoy them. You and your wife could cuddle while you're listening to them." There was the echo of another message. Cuddle while you have each other.

I suppressed a smile so as not to embarrass him and accepted the CDs gratefully. Keith had learned something vitally important about marriage relationships in his rocky journey through family life. A lesson many men twice and three times his age have not. He saw the crying need for the closeness he had been denied. I prayed that men's eyes everywhere would be healed enough to see, to see this truth.

Keith gobbled down his pizza, took a long, hot shower and crawled into bed. Morning came and I rose early to go for milk and eggs. Alone in the car, a voice inside said, *Are you going to buy his ticket from here? He'll never make it by Monday morning, you know.* I recognized the voice. It was the same one who told me to pick Keith up on my way home the night before.

The interior dialogue went this way: "I've done a lot for the kid already."

Answer: *What about Debbie?*

"I haven't got the extra cash and I can't help everyone."

You can *help him, and there's more where you got what you have.*

I pulled in at the bus depot and asked for the cost of the ticket. "That ticket will cost $175," the agent announced to me.

I deliberated, then in my indecision and reticence had a bold idea. I said to the voice, "If you clearly confirm that I should indeed buy this ticket, I will do it."

Telling the ticket agent I would think it over, I proceeded to the local supermarket. As I entered, two women were engrossed in conversation just ahead of me. As I came up beside them in the aisle, one turned to the other and said, "You wouldn't leave him stranded for a few bucks, would you?"

My knees felt weak. Those women will never know the ministry they performed by apparent coincidence that day. I bought my milk and eggs and returned to buy the ticket.

Keith was astonished by my generosity and profuse in his thanks. I didn't explain to him that I really felt I had no choice in the matter. He hesitated before boarding, fumbling for words of gratitude. As he fell silent, I said, "Would you like a hug?"

He held me with a hunger that moved my heart to the core. I hoped the hug would last him for a while. As the bus pulled away from the parking lot, I caught sight of Keith, his eyes focused on me with a mixture of joyful relief and unanswered questions. I knew inside that some of these would be answered by Debbie and her pastor.

My own anxious questions about my illness and my future had been answered by an awareness which filled me with a comforting love. Keith had delivered an unmistakable message of hope as I reached out to him. If I cared enough to help this stranger, wouldn't God, my Father, care for me, His son?

I looked again, and where Keith's face had been, I thought I saw the face of Christ. He focused His eyes on me, eyes of loving approval and I heard Him say, "Whatever you did for one of the least of these brothers of mine, you did for me" (Matthew 25:40).

13

When Time
Turns Golden

Y ou may have heard of Balaam's talking
donkey. If we are to believe this Bible story to
be literally true—and I do—then God spoke to Balaam
through his donkey. When the prophet stopped listening
to God's internal voice, God used the beast he rode on to
get his attention.

God spoke to me through a dolphin and encouraged my
father-heart through this miraculous visitation.

Although we receive reprieve from our daily grind and
relational stresses, we must remain vigilant and committed
to walking out our journey into wholeness rather than running and hiding from our struggles. We must walk into

the face of our pains, past, present, and future. When we run from pain and seek false comfort, we escape into fantasies from which we finally emerge, disillusioned and defeated.

Life with my family had become real and loving and nurturing. We were practicing honesty, integrity and repentance as a lifestyle. However, a broken relational history is ammunition for an enemy who abhors wholeness. He will use it to ensnare you with regrets and beat you with hopelessness. The battleground is your mind and only God can bring peace to that.

I believe there are times when God knows we are beyond human help. In mysterious but unmistakable ways, He crosses over a bridge of incredulity to meet us trembling on the other side. This is the nature of His love. We are indeed touched by angels to rescue us, to inspire us and to reveal God's eternal and personal love.

There are two such occasions—no, they were more than occasions. They were visitations which to my mind at least, communicated a tenderness beyond human expression. These memories remain like frescoes painted on the ceiling of my life and all I have to do is look up to see them in their beauty and feel His love all over again.

They both remind me that God will never love me more than He does today and never any less. They affirm that His love is unconditional, ever present and very, very personal.

You may not have my visitations, but God, who is utterly impartial by His very nature, tells you, "I am with you always."

It was the eyes of the dolphin which held my attention. They were brown, translucent orbs, and a flame seemed to flicker deep within, a buried light, seemingly of recognition. They saw what I had lost sight of long ago. The dolphin did not move; he seemed to wait for me.

Before I tell you what happened next, you deserve to know what I was doing in that place at that time and why our meeting changed my life.

Once or twice a year, I lose my way in my journey home to the celestial city of God. It seems that when I lose my way, my Guide searches for me. Once I am found, He and I, in some mysterious way, are able to make up the time that I have spent wandering in the desert of deception. The time is never wasted; He never wastes anything. It is, however, terrifying. It completely exposes my great need for the water of my Guide's presence. There is comfort in the knowledge that He will seek me until He finds me in my desert.

You see, I, along with the rest of humankind, have a history accessible by God and the devil alike. There is one profound difference in their individual ways of viewing my history, though. The sinful times that I would rather forget, God does not remember. It is not that He is unable to remember. He simply chooses to forget because He is gracious beyond measure.

The devil, that old serpent, is enraged by all this free grace and is powerless to change a thing. He parades my historical failures before me with impeccable accuracy. His malevolent purpose for this is to submerge my soul in the swamp of despair and block from my vision the smiling face of God's enduring love.

Of course, if the beleaguered believer, in the face of condemnation, would pause to reflect for even a moment, the truth would become obvious enough very quickly. What possible concern does the devil have about my holiness? Why, none, of course. Rather, he expends great effort to seduce me into sinning, then condemns me for having done so. He reminds me of a particular mean Mafia enforcer in one of the Humphrey Bogart movies of whom it was said, "He'll knock out your teeth and then shoot you for mumbling." The devil is a hateful fraud.

So, as I said, once or twice a year I allow that ancient foe to lead me down the paths of sightlessness for his name's sake. As he leads me ever deeper into the wilderness of discouragement, he makes claims of power which have no base in truth. But because of my pain and powerlessness, his claims of power seem valid. Oh, I put up a struggle all right, but the slough of despondency cannot support my frantic efforts to maintain my faithful footing. I sink, flailing and bemoaning the things I can never change.

The voice I now recognize as belonging to the snake begins innocently enough. *When you look back on your life, what would you have done differently? Most of your life is behind you now. What a shame you didn't change your ways a lot sooner!*

You've been given some valuable gifts, but what have you really accomplished with them? God must be deeply disappointed in you. So much wasted time. Four years of pastoral training, an excellent start in a church of your own, and now you're mowing lawns for a living. Sounds a lot like Peter going back to fishing.

Imagine . . . the very soul of hell feigning concern about my success at serving the Lord of glory! So deep and dark is his ability to deceive the human heart since Eden. So deep and dark my willingness to listen to him. He continues, his voice invading my thoughts, taking dead aim at my rising discontent.

He poses another question before I can answer first. *Isn't life and love rather backwards? You really seem to have found a peaceful harbor from the storms of life right now—personally, I mean—and your helping of distressed people is undeniable, I admit, but it's such a pity to have had all those years of conflict with your wife and the kids, isn't it?* The ploy seems obvious, but I feel the sting of loss injected by his words.

How old are you now? Fifty? Well, better late than never, I guess. It seems your kids were the ones who suffered the most from your self-focused life. You know what they say—the way a child is related to in his formative years is the way he will be in his own family. History repeats itself. Have you noticed the struggles your children are having of late? Why do you think your godly example isn't having any impact? I smelled sulphur as he hung over my shoulder, close and sinister, leering at the discomfort he sensed in my soul.

Having resisted taking his bait until now, I relent and enter the conversation for the first time. "I acknowledge that my contemptuous and wounded and defeated behavior affected Pearl and the kids big time."

Ri-i-ight! Drawn out and guttural, his voice went sliding into a modulation of smug satisfaction. *There's likely not a lot you can do about that now, is there?* He leads me further into the burning sand. *It's quite obvious to me that a lot of their respect for your thoughts, your opinions—and you—have eroded. Have you noticed how your children politely wait for you to say your piece, don't comment and move on to change the subject?* He let the implied accusation hang there while I morosely pondered the truth of his words. Then I leaped into the conversation gap, confessing on the run.

"That's what I call 'hangover.' My children fear that I will lapse into the teacher-lecturing mode of scolding and correcting everything that's wrong with the world. They lived with it for years and they learned to tune me out. I don't blame them one bit. The children haven't realized yet that I know what I've done and have repented of relating that way anymore. I'm on a new road now."

The braggart from hell swaggers at my side and snorts disdainfully. *Oh, I know you've changed . . . for now, anyway. Like I said, it's really sad when you think of the incredible times you could have today if all that hadn't happened. You may have noticed your friends' family, the ones who don't attend church. You know, Tom and Jennifer's family. Now* that's *communication. They are relaxed, intimate, and loving, sharing their thoughts with each other. I noticed they could disagree without becoming defensive, and like I said, they don't have any personal faith in that God of yours.*

He smirked as he noticed my eyes glaze over. *You can always dream, Clint. You can always dream.* I was losing ground, but my adversary wasn't done with me.

They say that a parent ignored in his prime is lost with the passage of time. Out of sight (perhaps in a senior's home), out of mind. But, hey, there's always heaven, right? This time the long, drawn-out graphic images of my withered and wasted frame slumped in a wheelchair in a hallway somewhere held me in a grip of fear.

Well, listen . . . His voice, just as crafty but fading to a hoarse whisper, drove in the final, fiery dart. *Whatever you didn't do back there, you can help others do now for themselves and their families. There's only one major obstacle. A man is believed for what he's done, not for what he says. When you've helped others, you still have to live with your own situation, don't you?*

I fell parched and exhausted in the hot dunes of my memories, endlessly and hopelessly stretching before my eyes. My eyes were looking backward and forward, searching for a sign of my Guide, longing for His water. I had tasted His water before. It was always offered me when I was most thirsty, most weary, most wasted. It was always held out by Him I recognized as the One I longed for the most. His hands are oversized, scarred and gentle. They are able to crush, but inclined to care.

And so I waited, wanting those hands to hold His water to my lips, wanting His eyes to find me. I listened for His calling voice, but the only sound to be heard was the shrieking wail of a demon in the distance, exulting in a job well done.

I came into focus as the trainer at Sea World received the applause of the crowd. He stood, arms extended, beaming astride the massive head of Shamu the killer whale. Explosions of fireworks signaled the grand finale of another day at Disney World nearby.

"Shall we go?" Pearl tugged at my jacket sleeve as I absentmindedly remained seated.

"Yeah, I'd like to get back to the hotel," I murmured. *Get back and get lost in the fantasy of a movie where things turn out okay,* I thought to myself. *Some water is better than no water, I guess.* I was tired from the struggle which had enveloped me. *Too tired to fight anymore. Who needs it? Not I. Let it go and carry on. I'm not the only guy who ever blew it. Forget the introspection and reflection. Press on, press through, kiss it goodbye and do what you have to do.* Anesthetized by the pep talk I had just given myself, I directed my attention to the crowds of people massing about me, heading for the exit of the amusement park.

I took up speaking to myself where the snake left off. *You are one of many thousands in one little amusement park, in one city, in one country. Oh, God, the insignificance of it all!* The brilliance of the fireworks mocked the black destitution of my heart as I moved toward the gate.

"Clint," Pearl pulled my arm as she headed for the dolphin petting pool. "We're just going to stop here for a few minutes," she said. Pearl loves dolphins and wanted to try with hundreds of others to feel their glossy skin as they raced around the Olympic-sized pool. A low brick wall was all that separated the curious onlookers from these exquisite creatures.

I marveled at their obvious enthusiasm in captivity. Deprived of the endless reaches and depths of the sea, they swam exuberantly within the tight perimeters of their tank. Formerly free to frolic and feast on an abundant variety of sea life, they were now fed out of a pail by their jailer with the same dead bait day after day. Once breaking the surface of the sea with great arcing leaps of utter abandonment as the setting sun turned them copper, they now endured the gaping, groping crowds. They too were powerless to change their past.

The trainer blew his whistle. On cue, the dolphins swam effortlessly, smoothly and obediently around the large enclosure. They were an arm's length away as they passed by. Many in the crowd reached out to touch their silky bodies. I tried, but without success. Others had better luck. I wandered off to try again on the far side of the pool, far away from the trainer's whistle.

The whistle sounded again and the dolphins gathered around the trainer to be rewarded for their performance. He fed the dolphins, gave two more sharp whistle blasts and off they swam to complete their required circuits. I waited without effort to touch them as they raced by me again. I was giving up.

A dozen or so of the fast-moving dolphins flashed by me in a frothing spray. They moved on. Astoundingly, however, one of the beautiful creatures rose up before me. He was mostly out of the water, almost stationary and well within arm's reach. Water trickled down his rubbery nose. His eyes, those luminous orbs, were fixed on mine and I sucked in my breath as did those around me. My heart beat hard in my chest as I sensed much more than the presence of a man-trained mammal.

My eyes saw, for a moment at least, but my mind could not grasp, what remained inconceivably before me. Out of the dolphin's mouth, clenched between his large and orderly teeth, hung a gold watch. I froze in fascination. Then—how, I cannot say—my hand reached out and took the timepiece from him.

It is easy to recall the smell of the briny water dripping from the dolphin and even now I can hear the metallic scraping as I removed the watch from his mouth. With a final penetrating look, my messenger—for that is what he was—slid silently beneath the water, heedless of the insistent whistle of his trainer. The dolphin had ears only for the bidding of his Creator. As he disappeared from view, the crystal-clear voice of my heavenly Father spoke. *My son, will you believe that I can restore time to you any way I please?*

My prison doors flew open! My mind was ablaze with revelatory light. My heart leaped from its grave and my eyes flowed with hot tears of gratitude. The Lord needs very few words to make the ones He created understand. He only needed three to raise Lazarus from the dead. I wept with the unshakable logic of eternity that came to rest inside my heart that night. I say "inside my heart" because the mind cannot contain nor process the truths of Almighty God tutored to a broken man. "With the heart man believeth unto righteousness" (Romans 10:10, KJV).

You're right, I said silently to the unseen One. This time the word "right" was uttered brokenly, but confidently and fearlessly.

And so He touched me that night through one nameless creature whose instincts were preempted for the sake of intimate mercy for one little man, in one little amusement park, in one little city, in one little country.

Like blind Bartimaeus, my crying heart had reached His attentive ears. "Son of David, have mercy on me!" (Luke 18:38). His question came back to my cry. "Will you believe?"

Like Thomas, cynical and disillusioned, He had met me at the end of my fingers. It was as far as my faith could reach.

Like the father of the wasted prodigal, He ignored my bargaining and bantering to fall on my neck with kisses as I stumbled into His presence.

And like a sunset beautifies a rocky slope, my mind was aglow now with the irrefutable, loving presence of the eternal One who is the same yesterday, today and forever.

It was the night that time turned golden for me.

14   The Angel of St. Ignatius

I n an hour of darkness, in the drudgery of life, in the devastation of the trail, I believe I met an angel. Not a helpful person—an angel. I can't swear to this, but nothing else could have sufficed at that point in my life. If was God's mercy I'm certain.

The Bible says, "He shall give His angels charge over you to keep you in all your ways lest you dash your foot against a stone." We all get broken feet, smashing them against hard and unyielding circumstances. We fall from great heights of hope and joy as we slip or someone else pushes us over the edge of betrayal. When our hearts are firmly resting, trusting in God to keep us, we are not always rescued from danger or difficulty but our feet will not be broken. By faith we can resume our journey even if it should lead through the valley of the shadow of death. The result is that we don't fear evil. Evil is eclipsed by the caring shadow of the Almighty over us. You have to be close to cast a shadow and He is close to those who trust in Him.

The angel I met was not recognizable as such, at least not by my primitive perceptions. It remained for God to introduce us. When He did, my eyes were widely opened to His love.

Angels are God's messenger service. They enter the sensory realm of people who need an unmistakable visitation of love, a vision of eternal reality. He sends these unquestioning messengers to those who are lost behind their limitations and helpless in their humanity. Angels' words and ways are unmistakable to those who have experienced them. Angel visitations have a way of making believers out of skeptics.

Angels can materialize to enter the human sphere. They can touch, talk, wrestle, defend, comfort, sing, feed and eat, among other things. They can disappear when their mission is accomplished. Angels can be entertained by people unaware of who they are—a clear case for impartial hospitality if I ever heard one.

Every angel in the universe is subject to the Lordship of Jesus Christ. They are only His servants and not to be worshiped in any way. When they are sent as messengers of mercy, our fascination and worship belongs to the God of mercy. He is the one who seeks and saves those who are lost and finds them hoping, waiting, helpless in the dark corners of the earth.

As I write this, my thoughts find a time in my life when I had lost faith in mankind, let alone a sovereign God or the angels around His throne. My story begins late on a February afternoon, in a hurry to get home after a stressful day at the office. Traffic was heavy on the icy streets as I turned south on Osborne Street off Broadway Avenue. Winnipeg's winter was wearing on me, and the restrictions of rush hour were using up what little patience I had left. The pace slowed to parade speed and even pedestrians were passing me now.

The traffic jam seemed to symbolize the past year—full of futility. Thinking of ways to escape, side roads to take, I thought of abandoning the car of my circumstance and just walking. Away from commitment, away from responsibility, away from the drudgery of life.

Money had been scarce. Dependent on snowfall for income, we had encountered El Niño. Even the Christ child seemed to be against me. An hour earlier over coffee with my friend Joe, he had commented on the tension in my face.

"What's up? You look like a man on the run."

"Pretty close, actually. I'm running but I haven't found anywhere to hide. I'm scared spitless, Joe, and I'm angry."

He looked at me silently. "Oh yeah, at who?"

"Why did you say 'at who'?

"Because there's always a who behind a what."

"Really."

"Uh-huh."

Discernment was Joe's strong suit and he listened well. "It's obvious to me, Clint. I don't think this is as simple as a shortage of work, is it? There's something else bothering you, and it's changing you from the inside. Want to tell me about it?"

It was as far as his sensitivity would allow him to come. Staring at my coffee, I began to uncover the hurt and betrayal feeding my anger. "Joe, why do people who lay it out for God and others get dumped on? It seems the more I reach out to people in need the more my difficulties increase, while many living selfishly prosper and cruise through this life. It makes no sense at all. And it makes me mad."

"What brought this on? I thought you were keen on your work at the Conflict Resolution Center." He had stepped on an emotional land mine. He watched my eyes fill up. "This is obviously eating at you and you need to give it away. I'm your man."

"I know. You're right."

Then I told him the bitter truth. The reality which gnawed at my sense of justice consumed my thoughts each waking hour. The weight of a brother's sin on my shoulders.

I had met Dale at a Family Life Seminar. We had hit it off at once. His easy manner, intuitiveness and intelligent repartee were attractive to me. I had longed for a friend of his caliber for a long time. We spent hours together talking, planning, praying about some way to reach out to families in conflict. Together we bought a building and developed a conflict resolution program for it to house. The response was extraordinary. Many were helped.

Then I discovered something quite by "accident" which made my blood run cold and cut me to the quick. Dale had forged my signature to borrow money against the mortgage on the house. My investment had been stolen by my best friend.

The days following that discovery were saturated with pain. There was murder in my heart. My mind reeled with the mystery of how such contradiction could reside in one man.

"Oh God, how could he do such a thing to me?"

The money lost was only the tombstone marking the grave where our friendship lay buried. I was now angered by Dale's sin and by God's permissive will which had allowed this suffering in my life. I wanted, with all my heart, to walk away from God's will and the betrayal of my friend. To just curl up in a corner and deprive the world of my company. To make a vow: "This will never happen to me again. I'll see to it." I felt my heavenly Father owed me my inheritance and I was asking for it ahead of schedule. I had worked long and hard for nothing. It was my turn.

Joe had heard me out without a word, then reached across the table to take my hand. "I read something on a sign the other day."

Just what I needed—a slogan. That would sort me out. I looked out the window, only half listening to Joe.

"God will never take you where His grace cannot keep you."

"He hasn't even asked me to forgive him, you know. What if he never does?" (He never has.)

Joe continued, "The choice you need to make is for God's sake and yours, not Dale's. God deserves your obedience and you need your freedom. Your situation makes me think of what they used to do to murderers in Old England. They were punished by having a dead corpse tied to their back. They had to carry it till it rotted. If you carry this thing, it will only add to the pain you already have. It will influence everything you do."

"Joe, I feel as if I can't go on counseling people."

"You can and you will if you forgive."

The truth of Joe's words were indisputable, but my craving for justice and my unforgiving heart cooperated to sink me into a sulking silence.

"Let's go." I stood to leave.

Joe followed and we said good-bye. I watched him till he disappeared into the traffic.

Joe didn't understand. How could he? Very few people, in fact no one I knew personally, had been ripped off for $5,000 by their best friend.

I have.

The words cut into my thoughts with the precision of a surgical knife, but gently, somehow, it pressed softly into my mind. I felt held by what I had heard. *Who do you think owes Me more than Dale owes you?*

The question didn't require an answer, but I murmured, "I do."

That was it. No negotiation, no ancillary clauses, no probation period.

I wanted to say, "Let me think about it. I'm not ready to forgive." But He had inarguably exposed me as a debtor just as fraudulent as the one whom I had imprisoned by my unforgiveness.

There was no escape. On one side lay the unscalable cliffs of unforgiveness. On the other a leap over the unknown precipice of God's unconditional love. I knew I had to choose. It was forgiveness or bondage.

Suddenly, horns blared behind me. I had been lost in my thoughts. The guy beside me yelled through his open window, "Won't get any greener, nimrod."

I stepped on it and cut him off turning west on River Avenue. Traffic was no better there.

How about St. Ignatius Catholic Church?

"What?" I was alone, talking aloud to my own thoughts. But the thought was strong and unmistakable.

Put up a poster for the Center at St. Ignatius.

I felt silly arguing with my own mind. "I'm not Catholic. I don't know anyone in that church."

My eyes picked up movement in my peripheral vision. A man had stepped off the city sidewalk and was walking in front of my car, hand held up as if to stop me. He was bareheaded, wearing a heavy mackinaw, jeans and work boots.

"I don't need this," I thought, rolling down my window to protest his intrusion.

As I pulled alongside him, he bent to look through my open window. I felt unable to speak. His eyes seemed blue yet crystal clear.

"Where are you going?" he asked.

There was a timbre to his voice which sounded odd coming from a person of his rather shabby appearance, and it sounded as if it were coming from a deep place, clear, melodic and strong. Each word seemed to contain more than the concept it conveyed.

"The church," I managed. "The St. Ignatius Catholic Church."

"So am I," he smiled, then deliberately walked to the passenger side of my car.

Stunned by his reply, I waited for my passenger to settle in. When he did, feelings rose up in me somewhere between excitement and fear. The inside of the car seemed charged with electricity.

We drove on in silence for a block. Looking straight ahead, I asked, "Why are you going to St. Ignatius?"

Without hesitation, he replied, "I'm a caretaker there."

Somehow it seemed right, as if I thought he would say that.

More driving, more silence. I sensed him staring at me. Turning, I looked into those smiling blue eyes again. This time a sense of love came to me so powerfully that my tears began to flow.

"That's a good work you're doing," he said.

I felt weak. My resistance to Dale, the people who clambered for my help, and God, who was letting me flounder, seemed to be melting away. I was unable to speak as we pulled up outside the church. Peace, like a blanket, covered and warmed me. My passenger got out without another word and entered the large doors of the sanctuary.

Taking a poster with me, I walked to the administration offices nearby. "Hi," I said to the receptionist at the desk.

"Hi," she answered.

"I just met your caretaker," I went on.

"Who?"

"Your caretaker."

She looked at me closely. "We don't have a caretaker."

I said nothing because everything had been said.

"That's a good work you're doing," I murmured to myself as I walked out. Then I added, "You just got to know who you're working for."

I got into the truck and glanced into my rearview mirror. The stone walls of St. Ignatius seemed warm and inviting. Maybe it was the presence of the stranger. Maybe it was the forgiveness and freedom glowing deep inside me.

In the parking lot, bowed over my steering wheel, the blood of Jesus paid for $5,000 worth of theft and a heart full of hate for the man who had called me friend.

"I release him, Lord," I prayed. "I forgive Dale. Forgive me for my hate and unforgiveness. He owes me nothing. I ask that your goodness draws him to repentance."

Something measurable lifted off me. My passenger, my messenger, had returned to me more than I had lost. Friendships unending, loyalty unswerving and the rich freedom of forgiveness.

"Thy Father, which seeth in secret shall reward thee openly" (Matthew 6:18, KJV). Maybe today or maybe one day, but He will. His will shall not take you where His grace cannot keep you. Joe was right.

The caretaker of St. Ignatius agreed with the Father and so do I.

Postscript

The Father-heart of God is constantly on my mind and heart. The bonding of my spirit with His grows stronger each day. My journey in search of my father has led me into ever straighter, more solid paths. I do not doubt His presence with me. As a husband, father, grandfather and man I can tell you there is no one who satisfies my deepest longings or loves me more than He. Reach out for Him, you will find Him waiting for you. No one who has ever done that has come away disappointed. He will be your Father too—and your friend—forever.